THE ROURKE DINOSAUR DICTIONARY

By

JOSEPH HINCKS

ILLUSTRATED BY
Gene Biggs
Mauro Cutrona
Gino D'Achille
Gabriele Menzioni

Rourke Enterprises, Inc.
Vero Beach, Florida 32964

Library of Congress Cataloging-in-Publication Data

Hincks, Joseph, 1949-
    The Rourke Dinosaur Dictionary

    Summary: Describes the physical characteristics and
habits of dinosaurs, arranged alphabetically from
Acanthopholis to Velociraptor.
    1. Dinosaurs-Dictionaries, Juvenile.   [1. Dinosaurs-
Dictionaries]   I. Biggs, Gene; Cutrona, Mauro;
D'Achille, Gino; Menzioni, Gabriele, ill.   II. Title.
QE862.D5H56   1989   567.9'1'0321   88-4612
ISBN 0-86592-049-4

INTRODUCTION

Fossil remains of dinosaur bones have been found all over the world. People have been collecting fossils for many centuries. Yet they have only recently come to understand the enormous variety found in the large family of dinosaurs. This dictionary describes 127 of the most interesting types. In all, scientists believe there were more than 300 different dinosaurs. Some were very similar to each other and it would have been impossible to tell them apart. The only way of knowing if they differed from each other would have been to compare parts of the skeleton.

The dinosaurs survived more than 160 million years but they died out suddenly about 65 million years ago. Nobody knows precisely why they vanished, leaving only their fossil remains. Scientists believe their disappearance may have been linked to sudden changes in the earth's climate. This in turn may have been caused by the impact of a giant meteorite hitting the earth and throwing up dust which could have brought cold, dark conditions for many years. Or, they may simply have died out as nature's way of replacing them with other life forms.

We should not think of dinosaurs as primitive animals with small brains and little intelligence. True, some had extremely small heads and could do little but munch plants. Others, however, were quick, intelligent and agile, moving quickly to snatch a meal or escape a predator. They were a very successful kind of animal with a wide range of different types and families that lived all over the world.

HOW TO USE THIS BOOK

This dictionary has been compiled to show the most common types of dinosaur known to have lived at some time during the Triassic, Jurassic and the Cretaceous periods. The section WHAT IS A DINOSAUR? explains the different families, how they can be distinguished from each other, and what made them so different from other animals. In THE AGE OF THE DINOSAURS, a time scale shows how the different groups and family types spread and increased during the Triassic, Jurassic and Cretaceous periods. Finally, DINOSAUR SIZES helps show the relative size of common types of dinosaur compared to modern mammals.

While the dictionary can be used for reference it is written also to be read like a book, beginning at the first dinosaur and finishing at the last. References to other dinosaurs are shown in *italics* and these can be found under the appropriate letter. Finally, while every effort has been made to include the very latest information, scientists are always discovering new and exciting details about known dinosaurs and new ones. So use this book as a key to unlock treasure stores of knowledge. Learn about the different dinosaurs in this dictionary and always refer to it for basic information. But go off and find out more about the exciting world of dinosaurs for yourselves.

WHAT IS A DINOSAUR?

TYPES OF DINOSAUR

There were many types of dinosaur but among the most famous was the family of sauropods. These were large, four-footed animals with small heads, long necks, large bodies, and long tails. They had quite small brains with a special nerve box in their hip to control the tail and back legs.

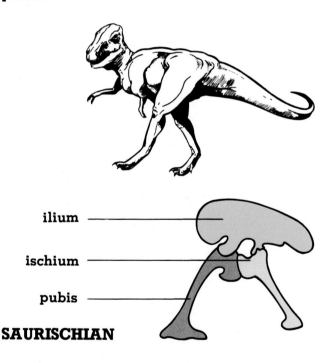

Heavily armored dinosaurs like this "node-lizard" ankylosaur were built for protection and combat. They walked on all fours and ate plants. Some were armed with large bony clubs at the end of the tail. Others just had side and back armor. Several types had spikes and plates.

Probably the most feared dinosaurs of all were the flesh-eating carnosaurs like *Daspletosaurus*. They walked erect on two legs; most had very small arms and weighed up to 7 tons. They could move quickly and would eat dead animals as well as killing other dinosaurs for food. All had large fangs.

DINOSAUR GROUPS

Whichever family a dinosaur belonged to, it was classed in one of two groups. The groups were distinguished by the way their hip bones were arranged. These bones are called the ilium, the ischium and the pubis. Saurischian (lizard-hip) dinosaurs had a hip bone arrangement like that seen in the drawing on the right.

ilium

ischium

pubis

SAURISCHIAN

Ornithischian (bird-hipped) dinosaurs had the hip arrangement shown in the drawing on the left. Here, the pubis lies back along the ischium instead of extending downward. In some later dinosaurs, the pubic bone extended beyond the ilium. That is the type shown here. All ornithischians were plant eaters.

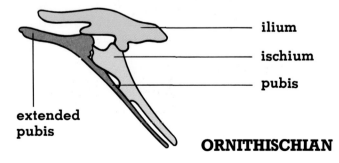

ilium

ischium

pubis

extended pubis

ORNITHISCHIAN

4

THE DINOSAUR WALK

The dinosaur was distinguished by the way its legs were attached to its hips. In the drawings below you can see the squat arrangement of a lizard, the semi-raised posture of a crocodile and the fully developed structure of a mammal or a dinosaur. The way the hip joints developed is also shown. We must not think of dinosaurs as primitive. They were highly developed.

LIZARD

CROCODILE

DINOSAUR

REPTILE

PRE-DINOSAUR

DINOSAUR

DINOSAUR FEET

Some dinosaurs walked on their toes, like *Ceratosaurus* whose leg and foot is shown in the left-hand drawing below. Other dinosaur feet, like those of *Apatosaurus* at bottom right, were adapted for carrying great weights across firm ground. It is wrong to think of giant sauropods like these wallowing in marshy swamps. Studies show they would have become hopelessly bogged down!

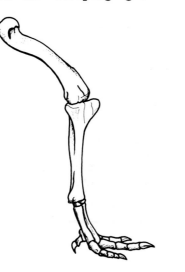

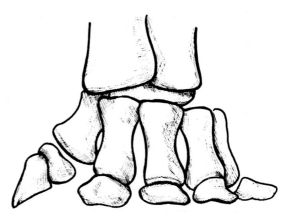

THE AGE OF THE DINOSAURS

SAURISCHIAN (LIZARD-HIP)

Dinosaurs of this type were found all over the world and lived from the middle of the Triassic period to the end of the Cretaceous. They were both meat and plant eaters, had clawed feet and included the families of sauropods (with five toes like modern lizards), carnosaurs (bipedal meat eaters) and coelurosaurs (similar to carnosaurs but with hollow bones, large brains and, possibly, warm blood). Reptiles and crocodiles are shown for comparison.

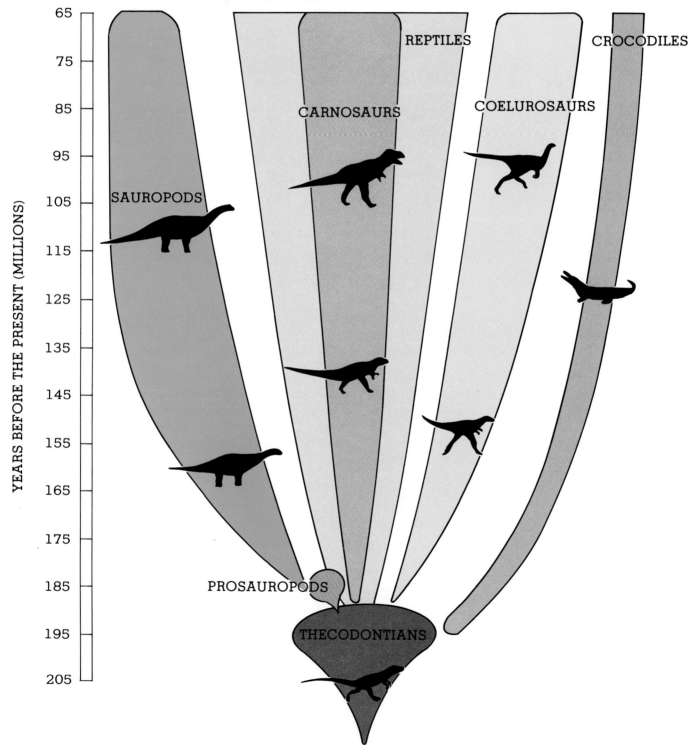

YEARS BEFORE THE PRESENT (MILLIONS)

65
75
85
95
105
115
125
135
145
155
165
175
185
195
205

REPTILES

CROCODILES

CARNOSAURS

COELUROSAURS

SAUROPODS

PROSAUROPODS

THECODONTIANS

ORNITHISCHIAN (BIRD-HIP)

These dinosaurs had hoofed toes, ate plants and most had beaked mouths. Some, like the stegosaurs and the ankylosaurs, had protective armor. Ornithopods were thought to have bird-like feet and ran with tails outstretched for balance. Pterosaurs were not true birds.

Modern birds are thought to have come from saurischian coelurosaurs. The ages of the birds and mammals are shown for comparison; like reptiles and crocodiles, they have survived to the present.

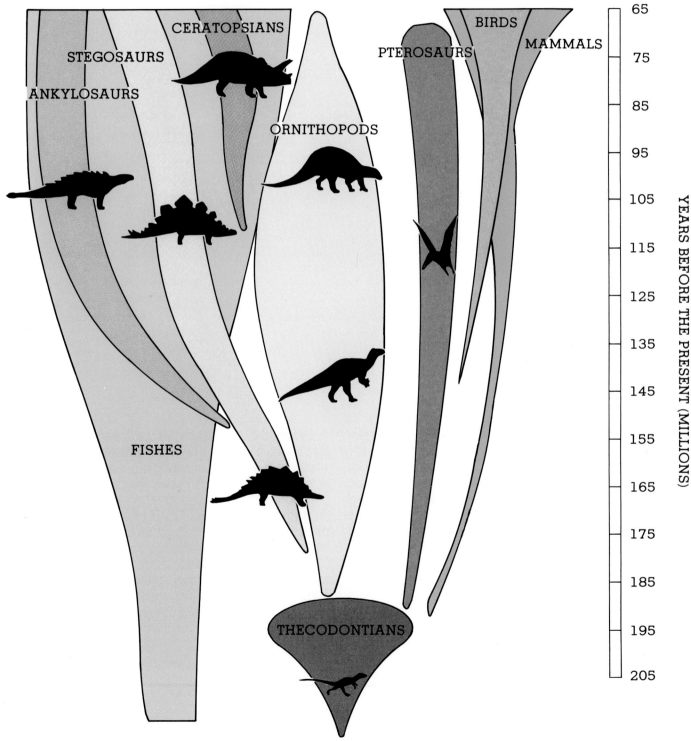

CERATOPSIANS

STEGOSAURS

ANKYLOSAURS

ORNITHOPODS

PTEROSAURS

BIRDS

MAMMALS

FISHES

THECODONTIANS

YEARS BEFORE THE PRESENT (MILLIONS)

65
75
85
95
105
115
125
135
145
155
165
175
185
195
205

Acanthopholis
(ā-kan-THOF-o-liss)

This dinosaur belonged to a family of ankylosaurs (armored dinosaurs). It lived around 100 million years ago, in the late Cretaceous period. Compared to other dinosaurs, it was quite small. Fossil bones found in southern England caused some scientists to believe Acanthopholis was about 17 feet long. Other scientists have put pieces of the skeleton together and believe it was only 14 feet long.

Acanthopholis was a plant eater. It roamed among shrubs and long grass looking for roots and small branches to nibble. Its front legs were shorter than its back legs, and so it could not reach plants higher than its raised head. Acanthopholis was built like a battle tank, with thick strong legs and a barrel-shaped body. It had an armored back made of bone slabs, plates, and spikes.

All ankylosaurs had small teeth set in small jaws. Each had a different type of tail, some with bony clubs at the end. Acanthopholis had a simple tail without any club. These animals were well protected from their enemies.

Acanthopolis means "thorn bearer." Not many pieces of this skeleton have been found, but it has been put into the group of nodosaurid ("node lizard") dinosaurs that had narrow snouts. Other family members included *Hylaeosaurus*, *Nodosaurus*, *Palaeoscincus*, *Panoplosaurus*, and *Silvisaurus*. All of these lived during the Cretaceous period.

Length: 17 feet
Weight: 2 tons
Lived: Late Cretaceous
Found: England

Albertosaurus
(al-BER-tuh-sawr-us)

Albertosaurus was a carnosaur. Carnosaurs were giant flesh eaters with big heads carrying powerful jaws and huge teeth. They had large bodies with powerful back legs and very short front legs. Albertosaurus had slightly longer front legs than *Tyrannosaurus*, a close relative.

Many skeletons of Albertosaurus have been found in the western United States and Canada, and in Mongolia. It is one of the most frequently found kinds of dinosaur fossils. For a long time, scientists thought that certain fossil bones discovered in different places were from separate kinds of dinosaurs. Now, they recognize them all as belonging to the Albertosaurus.

Because Albertosaurus was lighter than *Tyrannosaurus*, it was probably faster. Albertosaurus was about 16 feet tall. It had more teeth than *Tyrannosaurus* and could slash its way into the flesh of its victims, tearing them to pieces before swallowing them.

Length: 26 feet
Weight: 2 tons
Lived: Late Cretaceous
Found: North America

Allosaurus
(Al-uh-sawr-us)

Allosaurus is one of the most fearsome eating machines of the dinosaur age. Remains of these gigantic, flesh-eating dinosaurs have been found in North America, Africa, Australia, and Asia. In one field, scientists found remains of more than 40 Allosaurus.

Allosaurus had a head more than 3 feet long. With jaws hinged like those of a snake, it could swallow its prey whole. Its teeth were curved and up to 4 inches in length. Allosaurus was different from other flesh-eating dinosaurs. It had a ridge along the top of its skull and strange bumps above its eyes. The animal had powerful muscles and a strong tail to give it balance. With only small front legs it had to run and fight on its two powerful back legs. Allosaurus had a single claw 6 inches long on each finger. With these it could slash and tear the flesh of its prey. On each foot were three toes, each with a claw-like talon.

Allosaurus belonged to a family that lived successfully for about 100 million years. It would attack slow, lumbering dinosaurs like *Apatosaurus*. One fossil *Apatosaurus* skeleton has been found with Allosaurus tooth marks on its tail bones.

Length: 36 feet
Weight: 2 tons
Lived: Late Jurassic
Found: North America, Africa, Australia, Asia

Altispinax
(al-tuh-SPY-nax)

This unusual dinosaur lived over 120 million years ago. Fossil bones have been found in England, and it is likely that the animal roamed throughout Europe. Altispinax means "high thorn." Its name comes from the large spines on its back. Each spine was four times longer than the individual back bones it was attached to. A skin probably covered the spines, giving the dinosaur a sail-like fan across its back.

Altispinax was not as big as others in its family. With a length of about 25 feet it was not as big as *Spinosaurus*, which was 40 feet long. All members of this family were flesh eaters. They had sets of small, very sharp teeth. Like other flesh eaters, Altispinax had strong back legs and small, short arms. The sail, or back fin, probably helped the animal cool down in hot climates. Some scientists believe it may have been used to frighten other animals.

Length: 26 feet
Weight: 3 tons
Lived: Early Cretaceous
Found: Northwest Europe

Anatosaurus
(ah-NAT-uh-sawr-us)

One of the last dinosaurs to become extinct, Anatosaurus lived 65 million years ago. Anatosaurus was a duckbill dinosaur and belonged to a family that had jaws shaped like a duck's beak. They were called hadrosaurids and lived for more than 60 million years. Anatosaurus was a typical hadrosaurid. It had up to 1,000 tiny teeth in its mouth for munching vegetation. Many types of Hadrosaurids had a crest, each type shaped differently. Anatosaurus had no crest, but had instead a smooth, rounded head. Anatosaurus had strong back legs and could probably run very fast.

Anatosaurus was built to eat plants, leaves, and small shrubs. One set of remains has been found with pine needles in its stomach, along with seeds and fruit! They could stand erect on their back legs and nibble high branches or rest on their front legs and munch plants. If threatened, they could probably rear up and dash away at great speed. They had strong tails that provided balance when they were running on their back legs. Some Anatosaurus remains have been found with pieces of skin preserved. This is a very unusual find, and scientists have studied the skin carefully. Anatosaurus skin had a pebbly texture, like the skin of a lizard.

Length: 30 feet
Weight: 3 tons
Lived: Late Cretaceous
Found: Canada

Anchiceratops
(ANG-kee-sair-a-tops)

Anchiceratops was on earth for only a few million years, beginning about 69 million years ago. Like all the other dinosaurs, it became extinct 65 million years ago. Anchiceratops belonged to the ceratopsian (horned dinosaur) family and was about 17 feet long. All ceratopsians had a frill made of bone growing from the back of the head. Attached to the frill were very powerful muscles that worked its big jaws. Anchiceratops had a particularly large frill and a massive parrot beak. Three horns grew along the top of its face, two above its eyes and one on its beak.

Anchiceratops roamed the vast plains of Canada during the Cretaceous period, when lush vegetation was plentiful. It liked to crunch tough roots and probably grazed in large herds. They did not eat meat but their tough hides would have protected them well. Only vicious flesh eaters like *Tyrannosaurus Rex* would have been a match for Anchiceratops.

Length: 19 feet, 6 inches
Weight: 7 tons
Lived: Late Cretaceous
Found: Canada

Anchisaurus
(ANG-kee-sawr-us)

This little dinosaur was one of the first to appear on earth and dates back more than 210 million years. Anchisaurus was about 6 feet long and was built to move quickly on all fours. It had a small head and teeth shaped like diamonds. Nobody knows whether it preferred plants or meat. Some scientists think it ate both. Anchisaurus had strong legs and claws on each thumb. It probably used these to pull branches from small trees or flesh from small animals.

Anchisaurus weighed only 60 pounds and would have been able to run away from other animals that might have attacked it. Many fossil remains have been found all over the world. It is known as a prosauropod (lizard foot) dinosaur. Prosauropods led eventually to the biggest dinosaurs of all – *Brachiosaurus* and *Diplodocus*. Fossil remains of Anchisaurus were among the first ever found in North America. They are important because they help piece together the story of the origin of dinosaurs in many parts of the world. Anchisaurus is known to have lived in Europe and South Africa. It may have been seen all over the earth at the dawn of the dinosaur age.

Anchisaurus means "near lizard," and it got that name because its body was close to the ground. *Thecodontosaurus* was another member of the same family but had a narrower, longer head with fewer teeth. Fossils found in Australia may have belonged to Anchisaurus.

Length: 6 feet
Weight: 60 pounds
Lived: Late Triassic/Early Jurassic
Found: Northeast United States, South Africa, Europe

Ankylosaurus
(ang-KILE-uh-sawr-us)

This was the largest, heaviest, and most heavily defended of the ankylosaurid (fused lizard) family to which it belonged. It was more than 32 feet long, weighed 5 tons, and had lots of armor plates over its body. Ankylosaurids were armored dinosaurs with short legs and barrel-shaped bodies. They had short necks and stood low on the ground. Bony slabs, plates, and spikes were set into its skin, under which the flesh grew thick like panels of leather. Dinosaurs of this type had small teeth and jaws with very little muscle power.

Ankylosaurus was one of the most successful of its family at surviving. A great many of them were around at the end of the dinosaur age. They had evolved from earlier types more vulnerable to predators. Several fossil skeletons have been found in Canada, and most seemed to have survived by hiding under their armor. Ankylosaurus had a large bony club at the end of its tail. With this, the dinosaur probably lashed out at flesh eaters, knocking them off their feet or crushing their skulls.

Length: 35 feet
Weight: 5 tons
Lived: Late Cretaceous
Found: United States, Canada

Apatosaurus
(ah-PAT-uh-sawr-us)

One of the largest dinosaurs that ever walked the earth, Apatosaurus appeared around 155 million years ago and was a member of the great sauropod (four-legged plant eater) family. All sauropods had stiff limbs and thick legs. Animals like these were slow, lumbering beasts that spent most of their lives eating leaves and large plants. Big animals need a lot of food to satisfy their hunger, and dinosaurs were no exception.

Apatosaurus was once called *Brontosaurus*, or "thunder lizard," because people assume it must have shaken the earth when it walked. After all, it did weigh more than 30 tons. Apatosaurus had a very long neck that stretched more than 20 feet from its shoulder to its head. Scientists used to think the head was small but recent discoveries have shown it to be quite large. It had small teeth shaped like pegs and spent a long time chewing its food. Because these dinosaurs had small brains, scientists used to believe they were stupid. Modern scientists now suspect that they were more intelligent.

Length: 70 feet
Weight: 33 tons
Lived: Late Jurassic
Found: United States (Colorado, Oklahoma, Utah, Wyoming)

Archaeopteryx
(ar-kee-OP-ter-ix)

Although many scientists do not consider this a dinosaur at all, others think it was. Its name means "ancient feathers," and it is the earliest known animal to have feathers like a bird. The collarbone and some hip and foot bones, though, are more like dinosaur bones. Archaeopteryx had small muscles and three claws on each foot, with three-clawed fingers half way along each wing. Unlike birds, which have no teeth, this animal had small teeth. It also had scales on its face. From these facts it is possible to show that Archaeopteryx could not have flown very well. It would have fluttered around just above the ground like a frightened chicken.

Archaeopteryx is believed to be the link between land dinosaurs and true birds. For that reason, some scientists claim it is not a dinosaur at all, but the first real bird. It probably got its feathers from scales that split and allowed air to pass through. This would help Archaeopteryx get airborne – but just barely! It was probably descended from *Compsognathus*, which had a long neck, a very long tail, and light bones, just like Archaeopteryx.

Length: 3 feet
Weight: 20 pounds
Lived: Late Jurassic
Found: England, southern West Germany, United States

Avimimus
(a-vee-MY-mus)

This bird-like dinosaur appeared more than 70 million years ago and probably had lots of colorful feathers and fur. It was about 4 feet long, although some may have been as long as 5 feet. Avimimus would not have weighed much. It had small bones and little flesh. Its name comes from two words. One word, in Latin, means bird, while the other, in Greek, means to copy. It is called Avimimus because it looked like a bird, and some scientists first thought it was.

Avimimus was discovered in 1981 by a Russian who thought it truly was a bird. Later work by the same scientist showed it could only run on its back legs and that it could probably not fly at all. Nevertheless, it had feathers and was one of the early bird-like dinosaurs that are ancestors of today's birds. In some ways it was rather like a chicken. It probably ran furiously across the ground, snapping at insects or flying beetles.

Bactrosaurus
(BAK-truh-sawr-us)

Bactrosaurus is a duckbilled dinosaur that appeared nearly 80 million years ago. It is known to have had strong limbs and to have walked on its back legs. Bactrosaurus belonged to a family that evolved in Asia and included *Corythosaurus* and *Lambeosaurus*. Many scientists believe that a later member of the same family, called *Parasaurolophus*, developed from Bactrosaurus. Duckbilled dinosaurs of the Cretaceous period liked to eat plants and shrubs. They had powerful jaws for chewing food and could store unchewed food in their big cheeks. Their long tails helped balance them when reaching up for foliage or long shoots from small trees.

Nobody knows what Bactrosaurus had on the top of its skull. Only part of a Bactrosaurus skull has been found. Dinosaurs of this type were the first duckbills known to have walked the earth. They probably had smooth skulls without the bony crests later members of the family would have.

Length: 3–5 feet
Weight: 25 pounds
Lived: Late Cretaceous
Found: Southern Mongolia

Length: 13—20 feet
Weight: 1 ton
Lived: Middle Cretaceous
Found: Central and East Asia

Bagaceratops
(bah-gah-SAIR-uh-tops)

A ceratopsian (horned dinosaur), this little plant eater was only 3 feet long. He was an earlier member of the family to which *Anchiceratops* belonged. Bagaceratops had a relatively small face with a parrot-like beak. This helped the animal tear up small roots and shrubs to eat. He had no teeth.

Horned dinosaurs are famous for their neck frills made of bone and their several large horns. Bagaceratops had only one small horn just above its beak. It also had a small neck frill and would have been easy prey for flesh-eating dinosaurs. Bagaceratops has been found in Mongolia, and it is not known if they were common throughout the world. Compared to other horned dinosaurs, Bagaceratops looked like a small rhinoceros and may have lived in small groups for survival. Unlike other horned dinosaurs, Bagaceratops could not stand on its back legs.

Length: 3 feet, 3 inches
Weight: 1000 pounds
Lived: Late Cretaceous
Found: Mongolia

Barapasaurus
(bah-RAH-puh-sawr-us)

Barapasaurus means "big leg lizard" and is a combination of Indian and Greek words. It is called Barapasaurus because it had large legs. Unlike most other sauropod (lizard feet) dinosaurs, Barapasaurus did not have thick legs. Its limbs were long and slim, and it had a short head and spoon-shaped teeth. Some scientists believe it should belong in a family of its own. [Most put it among a group of lizard-foot dinosaurs separate from other groups like *Diplodocus* and *Brachiosaurus*.] The most notable difference between Barapasaurus and other sauropods is that it had longer legs, a taller neck, and a comparatively shorter tail. Scientists used to think dinosaurs like these spent all their life in lakes or rivers. They now think Barapasaurus lived by grazing and eating almost continuously. Dinosaurs like Barapasaurus first appeared almost 200 million years ago. They led to large numbers of giant plant eaters found all over the world. Barapasaurus probably died out around 150 million years ago.

Length: 60 feet
Weight: 28 tons
Lived: Early Jurassic
Found: Central India

Brachiosaurus
(BRAK-ee-uh-sawr-us)

This dinosaur has a length of more than 75 feet. It is one of the biggest ever found. The first Brachiosaurus was discovered in 1900 at the Grand River Valley, Colorado. When scientists put its bones together they discovered that its front legs were much longer than its back legs. This is why they called it Brachiosaurus, which means "arm lizard." All other dinosaurs had their longest legs at the back.

Brachiosaurus has a very long neck and a small head with little teeth. Its back is strong and arched with a relatively short tail. Brachiosaurus was very bulky and probably weighed more than 75 tons. It could have looked over the top of a three-story building and probably munched vegetation from tall trees.
Some people used to think Brachiosaurus lived in water, keeping only its long neck above the surface. Scientists now think it roamed around on land. It may have had a long trunk from the two big nostrils on the top of its head. No one knows for sure. Its been 130 million years since Brachiosaurus roamed the earth, and only the bones have survived.

Length: 70–90 feet
Weight: 80–100 tons
Lived: Late Jurassic
Found: United States (Colorado), Algeria, Tanzania

Brachyceratops
(brak-ee-SAIR-uh-tops)

One of the smallest of the short-frilled ceratopsids (horned dinosaurs), Brachyceratops has been named from a group of only five fossils. These were found together in one place in Montana. Each dinosaur was about 6 feet long. Some scientists thought they were not just small ceratopsids. They thought they were baby *Monoclonius* dinosaurs. The bones certainly looked like them and had the same features. Then the fossils of an adult were found, and now most scientists agree that these five examples represent a special type within the family of horned dinosaurs.

Brachyceratops had a very short neck frill made of bone. It was not unlike *Bagaceratops*, although it had two horns above its eyebrows in addition to a large horn on its nose. Brachyceratops lived about 75 million years ago, or 4 million years after Bagaceratops. It may be an early member of the family that led to *Monoclonius* and the giant *Triceratops*. All these were short-frilled dinosaurs.

There were many members of the short-frilled ceratopsian family, including *Centrosaurus, Eoceratops, Monoclonius, Pachyrhinosaurus* and *Styracosaurus.* All had horns, short neck frills made of bone, and scaly skins. Some had holes in their neck frills, while others did not. Some members of the family had bony spikes, and all known members of the family came from North America. Of course, it is always possible that some fossil remains may be found outside this region, but it is unlikely.

Length: 6 feet
Weight: 500 pounds
Lived: Late Cretaceous
Found: United States (Montana), Canada

Brontosaurus. See *Apatosaurus.*

Camarasaurus
(KAM-uh-ruh-sawr-us)

In several ways, Camarasaurus is similar to *Brachiosaurus*, except it is smaller. Like all other dinosaurs (excluding *Brachiosaurus*), its back legs are longer than its front legs. It has nostrils on top of its head, its neck is fairly short, and it has a deep skull and small teeth. The discovery of baby Camarasaurus fossils has helped scientists understand how dinosaurs looked as they grew up. When born they had big heads, short necks, and stubby tails. They changed as they developed.

The brain of Camarasaurus was small compared to its body. Its nose was on top of its head, just in front of its eyes. These dinosaurs must have led a lazy, peaceful life. Their size and tough hide would not make them good prey for flesh eaters, who probably left them alone. Camarasaurus probably wandered through the swamp and forest continually munching. Its little mouth had to feed a very large body.

Length: 60 feet
Weight: 20 tons
Lived: Late Jurassic
Found: United States (Colorado, Oklahoma, Utah, Wyoming)

Camptosaurus
(KAMP-tuh-sawr-us)

This one animal gave its name to an entire family of dinosaurs called "bent lizards" (camptosaurids). They are known to have lived more than 140 million years ago, during the late Jurassic period. Camptosaurids had strong back legs with hooves on their feet. This allowed them to run away from trouble quickly. Camptosaurids are named for their thigh bones, which were bent. They would sometimes stand erect and use their long tongues to pull leaves and foliage from shrubs.

Camptosaurus varied in size from 4 feet to nearly 20 feet. It had a small horned beak with which it could cut leaves and thin branches. Like many other dinosaurs, Camptosaurus could breathe while it chewed. This was possible because the passage that led from its mouth to its stomach was different from the passage that led from its nose to its lungs. Camptosaurus has been found in Europe and North America. It was an ancestor of the family of *Iguanodon*. It was more primitive, however, with four toes on each foot and without a spike on its thumb.

Length: 23 feet
Weight: 1,100 pounds
Lived: Late Jurassic/Early Cretaceous
Found: Western Europe, western North America

Centrosaurus
(SEN-truh-sawr-us)

This dinosaur belonged to the family of short-frilled ceratopsians (horned dinosaurs). Others were the tiny *Brachyceratops* and the much larger *Monoclonius* and *Pachyrhinosaurus*. These were almost as big as Centrosaurus. Like *Monoclonius*, Centrosaurus had a single horn on the top of its nose that curved forward instead of back. It also had a bumpy frill with two pieces of bone shaped like hooks. Centrosaurus had small hooves like a rhinoceros and very thick legs. Each back leg had four stumpy toes and each front foot had five "fingers." Centrosaurus had very strong jaw muscles to help it grind tough food. Scientists believe Centrosaurus traveled in herds. A single fossil find of eighteen separate animals has been discovered in Alberta. The most famous ceratopsian dinosaur is *Triceratops*. They lived mostly in great herds and roamed far and wide for root food and plants. In this way they must have been like great herds of bison ambling across the prairie.

Length: 20 feet
Weight: 2 tons
Lived: Late Cretaceous
Found: Canada (Alberta)

Ceratosaurus
(sair-AT-o-sawr-us)

Ceratosaurus means "horned lizard" and was so named because it belonged to an unusual family of horned flesh eaters. It is thought to have been related to *Allosaurus*, another flesh eater. But Ceratosaurus is the only dinosaur of its kind known to have had a horn on its nose. Ceratosaurus was up to 20 feet long and had a row of small, bony plates running down its back. It had short front legs with four fingers, each with a small claw. Each foot had three toes, also clawed. Ceratosaurus had a large head and a lightweight bone structure. Its teeth were shaped for tearing flesh and killing large animals.

Ceratosaurus probably hunted in packs. Scientists have discovered sets of Ceratosaurus footprints, suggesting that they roamed in groups. It probably lived about the same time as *Megalosaurus* but a long time before *Tyrannosaurus*, another flesheater. Dinosaurs like these would have been feared by all other animals. They were big and powerful and had large appetites.

Length: 20 feet
Weight: 1 ton
Lived: Late Jurassic
Found: United States (Oklahoma, Colorado, Utah), East Africa

Cetiosaurus
(SEET-ee-o-sawr-us)

This animal is one of the earliest plant-eating dinosaurs discovered. It probably lived at about the same time *Barapasaurus* roamed the earth. Cetiosaurus belonged to the same group of dinosaurs as *Diplodocus* and probably appeared around 190 million years ago. Scientists can tell that it is an early type, because its bones are not as well developed as other dinosaurs of its family. While others had lightweight back bones, hollowed out to save weight, Cetiosaurus had solid back bones. This observation helps scientists place Cetiosaurus several million years before *Diplodocus*, *Brachiosaurus*, and other types.

Cetiosaurus looked a lot like *Camarasaurus* and had a tail similar to *Diplodocus*. It was smaller than *Camarasaurus* and weighed about 10 tons. Cetiosaurus may have wallowed in rivers and lakes. Scientists are not sure how it lived. They think it probably went down to the water to cool off and wash just like the hippopotamus does today.

Length: 45–60 feet
Weight: 10 tons
Lived: Middle to Late Jurassic
Found: Western Europe, North Africa

Chasmosaurus
(KAZ-muh-sawr-us)

Chasmosaurus was a member of the ceratopsian (horned dinosaur) family and similar to *Anchiceratops*. Although smaller than its cousin, Chasmosaurus was a typical horned dinosaur. It had a large neck frill made of bone. Large holes in the bony plate reduced the weight of the neck frill. This made it easier for Chasmosaurus to move its head around. Strong neck muscles were attached to the frill. It needed these to pull out the roots of tough plants. Chasmosaurus had the parrot-like beak of other horned dinosaurs. The frill was longer than the skull itself and covered with skin.

Many Chasmosaurus fossil bones have been found in Alberta. Skin impressions on rock show it had small button-like scales all over its body. With these, its hide was probably quite tough.

Animals like *Tyrannosaurus* would have had a hard time trying to bite through its leathery skin. Their best defense would have been to run away!

Length: 17 feet
Weight: 3 tons
Lived: Late Cretaceous
Found: United States (New Mexico), Canada (Alberta)

Coelophysis
(see-lo-FISE-iss)

One of the very first dinosaurs, Coelophysis was known to have lived more than 210 million years ago. In 1947, scientists found more than a hundred skeletons at Ghost Ranch, New Mexico. There were many animals of different ages, and they ranged between 3 feet and 10 feet in length. This discovery has led scientists to believe that they lived in colonies and wandered about in large herds.

Coelophysis was a nimble dinosaur and could probably run very fast. It had slim legs, a long neck and tail and a pointed head with sharp teeth. Feeding on a diet of meat, Coelophysis had three fingers on each hand and a strong muscle joining its hips to its spine. This muscle probably enabled it to twist and turn as it ran, chasing small animals on which it fed.

Some fossil remains of a Coelophysis show babies inside what would have been its stomach. This causes some people to wonder if they were cannibals, eating their young when other food got scarce. Some scientists think they gave birth to live young. Other dinosaurs laid eggs.

Length: 10 feet
Weight: 65 pounds
Lived: Late Triassic
Found: United States (New Mexico)

Coelurus
(see-LURE-us)

Although Coelurus (hollow tail) first appeared around 160 million years ago, it was directly descended from *Coelophysis*. Coelurus was a small, nimble animal about 6 feet long. It had hollow bones for lightness and only three fingers on each hand. The thumb was short but the other two fingers each had a small claw. Coelurus was similar in appearance to *Ornitholestes*, another member of the same family.

Coelurus's head was slightly smaller than a man's hand. In its mouth were rows of small but jagged teeth. These helped it tear small pieces of flesh. Coelurus probably fed on small birds, tiny animals, and dead mammals. With its light weight and strong muscles, it could easily tear through the undergrowth, its head held low, grasping and snatching at wildlife within reach. Some of these small dinosaurs might have fed on the eggs of bigger dinosaurs. They may also have eaten berries or large seeds.

Length: 6 feet, 6 inches
Weight: 30 pounds
Lived: Late Jurassic
Found: United States (Wyoming)

Compsognathus
(komp-so-NAY-thus)

These small, fast running dinosaurs lived at the same time *Coelurus* was known to have been in North America. Compsognathus fossils have been found in Europe. They are among the smallest dinosaurs known. The adults were no more than 2 feet long, about the size of a chicken. They had long necks and very long tails. The stiff tail helped them run very fast and gave them balance. Each hand had two fingers and each finger had a claw. Their legs, twice as long as their arms, had three toes on each foot.

Compsognathus means "pretty jaw." Its long, pointed head held two rows of sharp teeth, and it is known to have eaten meat. It had hollow bones, which made it very light. Each animal probably weighed less than 7 pounds. This little dinosaur may have been an egg hunter. There would have been many eggs around in the dinosaur age. Some would have been large enough to provide a juicy meal for these nimble-footed animals.

It is hard to think of this little creature as a real dinosaur, yet he is as much a dinosaur as big *Tyrannosaurus* or giant *Apatosaurus*.

Length: 2 feet
Weight: 7 pounds
Lived: Late Jurassic
Found: Southern West Germany, southeast France

Corythosaurus
(ko-RITH-uh-sawr-us)

Corythosaurus, whose name means "helmet lizard," had a large crest on top of its head. Corythosaurus belonged to the family of duckbill dinosaurs called hadrosaurids. Among other hadrosaurid members were *Bactrosaurus, Lambeosaurus* and *Edmontosaurus.* Corythosaurus appeared after *Bactrosaurus* but just before *Edmontosaurus.* It was the only group of duckbills to have a crest on its head. The crest was hollow, narrow, and shaped like a dinner plate. Females and young had smaller crests than males.

Corythosaurus was probably used to feeding on small lizards, insect colonies, and plants. It had a toothless beak with which it would scoop up its food. From fossil remains it seems to have been about 30 feet long and probably weighed around 3 tons. Its big, heavy tail would be useful for keeping it balanced while it stood on its back legs and slowly munched food.

Length: 33 feet
Weight: 3 tons
Lived: Late Cretaceous
Found: United States (Montana), Canada (Alberta)

Dacentrurus
(day-sen-TROO-rus)

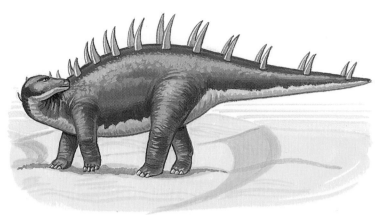

Dacentrurus belonged to the family of stegosaurid (roof lizard) dinosaurs; of which the most famous was *Stegosaurus.* Dacentrurus was only 15 feet long, about half the length of *Stegosaurus,* and weighed less than 1 ton. It was one of the earliest stegosaurids. Members of the stegosaurid family were divided into two groups. Some had bony plates down the top of the backs with spines on the tail. The others had mostly spikes and no plates. Dacentrurus had two rows of spikes along its back and tail. Because of its longer legs it stood higher off the ground than some other stegosaurids. Remains of this dinosaur have been found in England. Like other members of the family, it had three toes on each foot and four fingers on each hand. Dacentrurus had a small head and short teeth for eating soft plants. If attacked, stegosaurids would have little defense against meat-eating dinosaurs. They had large fleshy parts and no means of protecting themselves except with their spikes. If attacked, they could lash out with their spiked tail and damage a predator.

Length: 15 feet
Weight: 1,500 pounds
Lived: Middle to Late Jurassic
Found: England

Daspletosaurus
(dass-PLEE-tuh-sawr-us)

This dinosaur belonged to the family of tyrannosaurids (tyrant lizards). Others were *Albertosaurus*, *Tarbosaurus* and *Tyrannosaurus*, the most famous dinosaur of them all. Daspletosaurus, whose name means frightful lizard, was nearly 30 feet long from the tip of its tail to the end of its massive head. It weighed about 4 tons and had huge limbs with strong muscles. Although smaller and lighter than *Tyrannosaurus*, it had more teeth and was probably more agile.

This dinosaur appeared at the same time as *Albertosaurus*. It appeared earlier than *Tyrannosaurus* and *Tarbosaurus*. Daspletosaurus would have preyed on the ceratopsians (horned dinosaurs), like *Triceratops*, and the hadrosaurids (duckbills), such as *Parasaurolophus*. Scientists are not sure how fast the tyrannosaurids could run. Some think they were too heavy to move quickly. Of all the members of that family, Daspletosaurus would have been one of the fastest.

Length: 28 feet
Weight: 4 tons
Lived: Late Cretaceous
Found: Canada (Alberta)

Deinonychus
(dyne-ON-ik-us)

This dinosaur was one of the most efficient hunters of them all. It belonged to the family dromaeosaurid, or "running lizard." Terrifying flesh eaters like *Tyrannosaurus* would tear large dinosaurs to pieces with their huge teeth and massive jaws. Yet they could probably not move very fast. One dinosaur that could was Deinonychus. This dinosaur was the largest in his family, which also included *Dromaeosaurus* and *Velociraptor*.

Deinonychus means "terrible claw." It was given this name because it had a sickle-shaped toe and claw on each foot. The other three toes on each foot were shorter. When running it would lift the claw up and put the outer toes to the ground. The toe with the big claw would be used to rip the bodies of other dinosaurs. Balancing on one leg, it would slash viciously using strong muscles in its thigh. Its tail had long pieces of bone to make it stiff when running. Small arms and hands each had three clawed fingers. Deinonychus had a large head, good eyesight, and sharp teeth.

Length: 10–11 feet
Weight: 250 pounds
Lived: Early Cretaceous
Found: Western United States

Dicraeosaurus
(dye-CREE-uh-sawr-us)

A member of the same family as *Diplodocus*, this smaller relative appeared in the late Jurassic period, more than 150 million years ago. Dicraeosaurus was one of that large group of lumbering plant eaters that lived for more than 100 million years. It was only 40 feet long and stood 10 feet tall. Its name means "forked lizard" and refers to the bones that make up its spine. Some of its back bones are divided to look like a giant Y. The branches on top had large muscles attached to them. Unlike *Diplodocus*, Dicraeosaurus had solid back bones.

This dinosaur weighed about 6 tons and probably spent most of its life peacefully munching plants and lush vegetation. This peace could end, though, if it was attacked by one or more of the fearsome flesh-eaters. It had little or no defense and might have escaped by walking into deep water. Dinosaurs could not swim and would probably not go into rivers and lakes unless attacked. Large, four-footed ones could wade in and escape.

Length: 43–66 feet
Weight: 6 tons
Lived: Late Jurassic
Found: Tanzania

Dilophosaurus
(dye-LŌ-fuh-sawr-us)

This animal belonged to the megalosaurid (great lizard) family that appeared very early in the Jurassic period, around 200 million years ago. It was related to *Megalosaurus*. Dilophosaurus had a large head and two thin bony crests running from the top of its nose to the back of its head. These gave it its name, which means "two-ridged lizard." When first discovered, scientists thought the crest belonged to another animal because it was found some distance away from the skull. Later discoveries proved the crest came from this dinosaur.

Dilophosaurus had five fingers on each hand. The two inner fingers were very small. The outer fingers had long claws like fangs. These would have been used to lash out at victims, easily ripping into flesh. Its powerful jaws would have easily crushed flesh and bone as it sank its huge teeth into the animal's body. On its feet were three clawed toes and a small "big" toe turned backward.

Length: 20 feet
Weight: 1,500 pounds
Lived: Early Jurassic
Found: United States (Arizona)

Diplodocus
(dih-PLOD-uh-kus)

Diplodocus is one of the most famous of the four-legged prehistoric plant eaters. A complete skeleton of Diplodocus was dug up by the famous Scottish-American millionaire, Andrew Carnegie. It was 88 feet long, including a 26-foot neck and a 45-foot tail. The head was quite small and had two rows of peg-like teeth. These were used to pull leaves from tree branches like a comb rakes through hair.

With its long neck, the dinosaur could see over trees and across great distances. This was just as well. It would not have been a fast mover and proved an easy prey to the big flesh-eaters. Diplodocus weighed more than 11 tons. It needed a special skeleton to support that weight. The dinosaur takes its name, which means "double beam," from small bones beneath the backbone. These had a piece that ran forward as well as another piece that ran back – a double-beamed bone. Diplodocus is one of the longest dinosaurs that ever lived. It is not the heaviest. In fact, for its size, Diplodocus was light. Compare Diplodocus with *Apatosaurus*, which weighed 33 tons and yet was nearly 20 feet shorter in length.

Length: 87 feet
Weight: 11 tons
Lived: Late Jurassic
Found: United States (Colorado, Montana, Utah, Wyoming)

Dromaeosaurus
(drom-ee-uh-SAWR-us)

One of the dromaeosaurid (running lizard) dinosaurs like *Deinonychus*, but smaller. Fossil remains show it to have been about the size of a man and to have weighed approximately 100 pounds. Its tail was made stiff by rods of bone and helped keep it balanced when running fast. Dromaeosaurus had a large head which contained a big brain. The dinosaur would have been able to balance itself on one leg with the help of its stiff tail while savagely attacking its prey with its clawed toes.

Dromaeosaurus appeared later than its relative, *Deinonychus*, and stalked the earth in the late Cretaceous period, about 70 million years ago. Because Dromaeosaurus was so much smaller it probably had best pickings among the tiny animal life. Many small reptiles and mammals would have been attacked by this fast-moving dinosaur. Dromaeosaurus lived about the same time as *Velociraptor*, although it appeared earlier.

Length: 6 feet
Weight: 100 pounds
Lived: Late Cretaceous
Found: Canada (southern Alberta)

Dromiceiomimus
(dro-miss-ee-o-MY-mus)

This dinosaur belonged to the family of ornitho-mimids (ostrich dinosaurs). They were called this because they looked like ostriches with a long tail and no feathers. Unlike most other dinosaurs, ornithomimids were very fast. Nothing could catch them. At full speed, Dromiceiomimis was quicker than a galloping horse. It had a long slender neck and a large head. Although about 12 feet long, its thin, light bones gave it a weight of only 220 pounds. Its neck was long and slender, supporting a large head with a big brain and huge eyes. They had no teeth, but each foot had three toes. Each hand had three spindly fingers, each with a tiny claw.

Dromiceiomimus means "emu mimic." It was named this because it looked like an emu. The dinosaur was in the same family as *Ornithomimus* and *Struthiomimus*. Unless surprised while feeding, it is unlikely that the Dromiceiomimus was easy prey. It probably fed on seeds, small eggs, insects, or other pickings in woods and on plains. If disturbed, it would lift up its stiff tail, raise its head, and run quickly to safety.

Dromiceiomimus lived at the end of the great age of dinosaurs. Members of the ornithomimid family spanned 100 million years, from the mid-Jurassic to the end of the Cretaceous period. Most ornithomimids lived during the middle to late Cretaceous era. They represent the end of a long line of ostrich dinosaurs that began with the coelophysids in the late Triassic. The most famous coelophysid was *Coelophysis*, which weighed less than one-third the weight of Dromiceiomimus.

Length: 11 feet, 6 inches
Weight: 220 pounds
Lived: Late Cretaceous
Found: Canada (southern Alberta)

Dryosaurus
(DRY-o-sawr-us)

A member of the large group of "bird-footed" dinosaurs, this one belonged to a family known as the gazelles of prehistoric animal life. They were all small and quite fast, with five-fingered hands and four toes on each foot. They chewed plant food and vegetation with small teeth inside horny beaks. These were very successful survivors. The families in this group lived for more than 100 million years. They were among the first "bird-footed" dinosaurs to appear and lived among types like *Camptosaurus*.

Dryosaurus, which means "oak lizard," was the biggest of the group. Some were up to 14 feet long. A nearly complete Dryosaurus skeleton was found in Utah. From this scientists have discovered it had long, agile legs, which gave it speed when in a chase. It had little else to defend itself with. It would probably forage among vegetation and plant life, always bobbing its head up to watch for big preying flesh eaters!

Length: 9–14 feet
Weight: 120–180 pounds
Lived: Middle to Late Jurassic
Found: Eastern England, Romania, Tanzania, United States (Utah)

Dryptosaurus
(DRIP-tuh-sawr-us)

This animal is one of the most mysterious dinosaurs, because nobody has been able to build up a full skeleton. At least 12 fossil specimens have been found, however. The best skeleton was dug up by a famous dinosaur collector in 1866. He called the dinosaur Laelaps. Because somebody had already given that name to an insect it was changed to Dryptosaurus, which means "tearing lizard." This was an appropriate name. Dryptosaurus was a large meat eater like *Tyrannosaurus*. It was about 25 feet long with curved teeth and three large claws on each foot.

Some scientists think this dinosaur may have been a different member of the *Tyrannosaurus* family. Others think it was closely related to *Megalosaurus*. A few have even linked it with *Iguanodon*! The picture shows how Dryptosaurus might have looked when he roamed the earth around 70 million years ago.

Length: 25 feet
Weight: 1 ton
Lived: Late Cretaceous
Found: United States (New Jersey, Maryland, Colorado, Montana, Wyoming)

Edmontosaurus
(ed-MON-tuh-sawr-us)

This dinosaur was one of the giants in the large family of duckbill dinosaurs. It was as long as 43 feet and could weigh more than 3 tons. It belonged to the group of "bird-foot" families and appeared during the late Cretaceous period, about 72 million years ago. Edmontosaurus were plentiful: they were known to have lived all over the earth.

Edmontosaurus did not have a bony crest on top of its head, as other duckbills did. Its skull was low in front and high at the back. It fed on plants that needed to be chopped up before being swallowed. To do that it had about a thousand teeth in its soft mouth. Scientists know quite a bit about this dinosaur because they have found so many skeletons.

Some scientists think Edmontosaurus had flaps of skin on each side of its nose. When it blew these up like balloons, they made a loud bellowing sound. Like many other animals, dinosaurs probably used these loud noises to communicate.

Length: 33–42 feet
Weight: 2–3 tons
Lived: Late Cretaceous
Found: United States (New Jersey, Montana), Canada (Alberta)

Elaphrosaurus
(eh-LOFF-ruh-sawr-us)

One of the earliest ornithomimids (ostrich dinosaurs), Elaphrosaurus was a relative of *Dromiceiomimus*, *Gallimimus*, *Ornithomimus*, and *Struthiomimus*. It was probably one of the earliest members of that family and fossil bones have been found that date back to the late Jurassic period. Most "ostrich dinosaurs" are found from the Cretaceous period. A distant relative is *Ornitholestes*, a small dinosaur only half the size of Elaphrosaurus.

With long, slender legs and a stiff tail, Elaphrosaurus would have easily sprinted from danger. It had keen eyes and a quick brain. Its diet probably depended on where it lived. Near the sea it might have grubbed around for shellfish or shoveled sand for tiny creatures. Some lived far inland and others foraged among woods and forests. Since it had no teeth, Elaphrosaurus could not have eaten meat.

Length: 11 feet, 6 inches
Weight: 220 pounds
Lived: Late Jurassic
Found: Algeria, Tanzania, Morocco, Tunisia, Egypt, Niger

Eoceratops
(EE-o-sair-uh-tops)

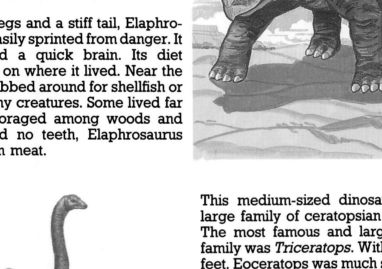

This medium-sized dinosaur belonged to the large family of ceratopsian (horned) dinosaurs. The most famous and largest member of this family was *Triceratops*. With a length of about 20 feet, Eoceratops was much smaller than *Triceratops*. Horned dinosaurs varied in size and had different types of horns. Some, like *Brachyceratops*, were no larger than 6 feet and had only one small horn. These appeared around 75 million years ago. *Triceratops* was huge and had three big horns, two of which were 4 feet or longer. *Triceratops* appeared about 67 million years ago. Eoceratops was an early horned dinosaur. It is thought to date back almost as far as *Brachyceratops* and is best known from fossil bones dug up in Alberta. Three small horns on its face crowned a 3-foot-long skull. A short bony neck frill protected the back of its head from the fangs of meat-eating dinosaurs. Eoceratops means "early horned face." It was probably the earliest of its family type.

Length: 20 feet
Weight: 2 tons
Lived: Late Cretaceous
Found: Canada (Alberta)

Erlikosaurus
(er-LIK-uh-sawr-us)

This flesh eater was found among remains dug up in Mongolia. It belonged to a strange branch of the big carnosaur (flesh lizard) group. Other families belonged to types like *Tyrannosaurus*, *Allosaurus*, and *Megalosaurus*. Erlikosaurus belonged to the family of "slow lizard," or segnosaurid, dinosaurs. It was named in 1980, and most scientists think it was a direct descendent of *Megalosaurus*. Erlikosaurus appeared late, more than 100 million years after *Megalosaurus* first walked the earth.

Erlikosaurus did not look like *Megalosaurus*, though. It looked more like *Deinonychus* in size, but had longer arms and smaller teeth. Its top lip ended in a toothless beak. It had four toes, each with a long claw. It is believed its feet may have been webbed like a duck's. Other members of the same family were even bigger than Erlikosaurus. One, called *Segnosaurus*, was 30 feet long and stood more than 8 feet tall.

Length: 13 feet
Weight: 280 pounds
Lived: Late Cretaceous
Found: Mongolia

Euhelopus
(you-heh-LO-pus)

One of the big plant-eating dinosaurs similar to *Camarasaurus*, Euhelopus, or "good marsh foot," had a longer neck and nose. Like *Camarasaurus*, it had strong teeth that grew around its jaws. Other dinosaurs of this type had teeth growing only in front. Euhelopus had large nostrils on top of its head. Because of this, some scientists think it had a long trunk. That would have made it look very strange. Both *Camarasaurus* and Euhelopus were camarsaurid (chambered lizard) dinosaurs, with hollow chambers in the backbone.

Euhelopus was a little slimmer than *Camarasaurus*, but large members of the family may have weighed as much as 24 tons. The biggest could have been up to 50 feet in length – without trunk. In this picture, Euhelopus is shown without a trunk. From fossil remains, scientists believed they were at home in marshy land at the bank of muddy rivers or in swamps. They would have been safer there than on dry or wooded land where the big flesh eaters roamed.

Length: 33–50 feet
Weight: 18–24 tons
Lived: Early Cretaceous
Found: China (Shantung)

Euoplocephalus
(you-op-luh-SEF-uh-lus)

Named for its "well armored head," Euoplocephalus was a member of the family of ankylosaurs. These "fused lizards" were best known by the bones of *Ankylosaurus*, the biggest of them all. There were at least twelve different types within the family and Euoplocephalus was typical in size and weight. It probably weighed nearly 3 tons and has been dug up in places as far apart as Alberta and Sinkiang, which is in northwest China.

All ankylosaurs were about the size of a modern battle tank. They had different arrangements of armored bands down their backs with ridged plates and blunt spikes. Euoplocephalus had round nostrils and a horny, toothless beak. Row upon row of armored back plates helped protect it from predators. At the end of its tail it had a large, bony club. Ankylosaurids were among the last dinosaurs to appear before all dinosaurs

became extinct 65 million years ago. Euoplocephalus was well adapted to munching plants and lush greenery while protected from attack.

Two closely related families of ankylosaurs were the "fused lizards" and the "node lizards." Both appeared from a common ancestor at the beginning of the Cretaceous period and have been found all over Europe, North America, and Asia. Node lizards included *Acanthopholis*, *Hylaeosaurus*, *Nodosaurus*, *Panoplosaurus*, and *Silvisaurus*.

Length: 23 feet
Weight: 3 tons
Lived: Late Cretaceous
Found: Canada (Alberta), China (Sinkiang)

Fabrosaurus
(FAB-ruh-sawr-us)

Fabrosaurids, or "Fabre's lizards" were among the earliest dinosaurs known. They were small, the largest as tall as a man, and light-boned. Fabrosaurus was only 3 feet long and had hollow limb bones with small arms and long legs. Each hand had five fingers and each foot had four toes. In its relatively small mouth were two rows of ridged teeth. With these, it could grind small roots and shoots. Fabrosaurus had a broad jaw with holes for new teeth to replace old ones.

Fabrosaurus was closely related to *Lesothosaurus* and *Scutellosaurus*. It appeared late in the Triassic period, more than 200 million years ago. Dinosaurs of the fabrosaurid family lived for at least 70 million years and were like the grazing animals of today. They would have been the gazelles and deer of the dinosaur world. From this line of ancient animals came *Heterodontosaurus, Hypsilophodon, Camptosaurus, Iguanodon, Hadrosaurus, Bactrosaurus*, and many other duckbills, boneheads, and other groups.

Length: 3 feet, 4 inches
Weight: 40 pounds
Lived: Late Triassic/Early Jurassic
Found: South Africa (Lesotho)

Gallimimus
(gall-ih-MY-mus)

With a long neck, bony tail, and strong legs for running, Gallimimus was the largest of the ostrich dinosaurs (ornithomimids). Its name means "fowl mimic" because it seemed to copy the behavior and appearance of certain fowls we know today, like the ostrich and the turkey. With a length of 13 feet, it could probably move quickly on its long legs. Other relatives were *Dromiceiomimus* and *Elaphrosaurus*. Gallimimus had poorly developed hands. They would not have been much use for grasping tiny lizards or tearing open insect nests. Each member of the family of ostrich dinosaurs differed in some way from its relative. Gallimimus had an unusually long snout with a broad, flat end.

Like other members of the family, Gallimimus would quickly sprint away from danger. With long loping legs, it would have looked like an ostrich as it ran. It may have snapped and pecked at dinosaur eggs. Dinosaur eggs were small with thin shells similar to chicken or turkey eggs. A good strong peck from Gallimimus' beak would have been enough to break them open.

Length: 13 feet
Weight: 250 pounds
Lived: Late Cretaceous
Found: Southern Mongolia

Geranosaurus
(jer-AN-uh-sawr-us)

This tiny dinosaur was a close relative of *Heterodontosaurus*, Geranosaurus was among the very first dinosaurs that appeared. They were ancestors of "bird-footed dinosaurs," such as *Fabrosaurus*. Scientists believe they eventually led to the great families of the bonehead dinosaurs like *Pachycephalosaurus*. More than 130 million years before the bonehead dinosaurs, however, the little Geranosaurus roamed large areas of South America and South Africa. At that time, the two countries were joined together. Since then, over millions of years, South America and Africa drifted apart.

Geranosaurus means "crane-lizard." It had tusks as well as teeth that were used for grinding food. Perhaps only males had tusks. Geranosaurus had small tusks in the lower jaw but no sockets for them in the upper jaw. It is believed these little dinosaurs died out around 200 million years ago. Heterodontosaurids did not lead to other, more developed descendents. Yet they came from a line that also produced the "bird-foot" dinosaurs, and scientists think they may still find remains of later members of the heterodontosaurid family. It would not be surprising if they turned up in South America.

Length: 4 feet
Weight: 50 pounds
Lived: Late Triassic/Early Jurassic
Found: South Africa

Hadrosaurus
(HAD-ruh-sawr-us)

This was the first dinosaur from North America to be named. Its bones were dug up in New Jersey, and in 1858 it was given a name that means "different foot." This became the family name for a large group of hadrosaurids. The family also included *Edmontosaurus*, which was much bigger and heavier than Hadrosaurus. All duckbills had flat heads with solid bone crests or humps on top. The shape and size of these features varied among different members of the family. Hadrosaurus had a deep, narrow face. It had two rounded humps, one above each eye socket. Scientists have discovered fossil remains of Hadrosaurus that date back 78 million years, making Hadrosaurus older than *Edmontosaurus*. In fact, they were not very closely related. Both came from an unknown ancestor believed to have been on earth more than 80 million years ago. Some scientists, however, think both types were much older than this. They have found fossil footprints 120 million years old that look just like those made by Hadrosaurus.

Length: 26—32 feet
Weight: 1 tons
Lived: Late Cretaceous
Found: United States (New Jersey, New Mexico), Canada (Alberta)

Herrerasaurus
(her-RAY-rah-sawr-us)

This fearsome meat eater belonged to the group of prosauropod ("before the lizard feet") dinosaurs. Prosauropods go back to the beginning of dinosaur life, 220 million years ago. From these different families came the great and gigantic plant eaters like *Cetiosaurus*, *Brachiosaurus*, *Camarasaurus*, and *Diplodocus*. Herrerasaurus was not the earliest prosauropod, but it was the biggest of its family. Its big head had two rows of teeth shaped like sickles. With long back legs and large front legs, it was probably able to move quickly across rough ground. Its front legs probably helped it climb across rocky land.

From bones dug up in Argentina, Herrerasaurus is known to have been about 10 feet long and to have weighed around 220 pounds. Others in the family have been found in China. Not many are believed to have existed. They did not seem to survive beyond the early Jurassic period, about 200 million years ago.

Length: 10 feet
Weight: 220 pounds
Lived: Late Triassic
Found: Northwest Argentina

Heterodontosaurus
(het-er-uh-DON-tuh-sawr-us)

A close relative of *Geranosaurus*, Heterodontosaurus was more advanced and larger. These small dinosaurs would have been on earth at the same time as *Herrerasaurus* and *Fabrosaurus*. All three kinds date back to the late Triassic, more than 190 million years ago. Heterodontosaurus remains have been found in South Africa, Argentina, and China. This animal had one thing in common with people: three different types of teeth. It had sharp, cutting teeth at the front, fangs at the front of the lower jaw, and molars in the back for grinding.

Heterodontosaurus had three toes on each foot and a claw at the back of its heel. It had five fingers on each hand. Like most other members of this family, Heterodontosaurus was small, about 4 feet long. Some of these dinosaurs had muscles in their cheeks. They probably had a mixed diet of small insects and plant roots, with seeds, nuts, and primitive forms of fruit. Heterodontosaurus had small, grasping hands that could forage and grub around for juicy food. There were no defensive weapons on its body. Only the speed of its legs would help it escape attack.

Length: 4 feet
Weight: 50 pounds
Lived: Late Triassic/Early Jurassic
Found: South Africa

Homalocephale
(ho-mah-luh-SEF-uh-lee)

Its name means "level head" because it had a flat top to its skull. There were several bumps on the top of its head and a pattern of small pits. Most remains come from Mongolia and it was probably about 10 feet long. Homalocephale was one of the large family of "bone-head" dinosaurs that lived about 70 million years ago. They are thought to have descended from the family of *Heterodontosaurus* dinosaurs, which lived more than 110 million years earlier. Homalocephale was closely related to *Pachycephalosaurus*.

Like other members of its family, Homalocephale had a very thick skull. This may have been used to attack others that tried to invade its territory, or it may have been used to play. Animals of today often butt heads in play. Homalocephale probably lived on high slopes and on the sides of mountains. Most of its fossil remains have been washed down from high places by fast-flowing streams. These animals walked on their back legs, using their tails as props when standing.

Length: 10 feet
Weight: 200 pounds
Lived: Late Cretaceous
Found: Mongolia

Hylaeosaurus
(hy-LAY-ee-uh-sawr-us)

This primitive ankylosaur ("armored dinosaur") was closely related to *Acanthopholis*. It lived about 120 million years ago and belonged to the "node lizard" group of ankylosaurs. The other group, called "fused lizards," included *Ankylosaurus*. Hylaeosaurus means "woodland lizard," and it was discovered in southeast England as long ago as 1833. It probably had spikes along the sides of its body and plates jutting up along the tail. Underneath, it had a heavily armored back from its head to its tail.

Unlike the "fused lizard" ankylosaurs, Hylaeosaurus and its relatives did not have a thick, bony tail club. Instead of hitting the attacking predator, it may have stood higher on its legs to run away at the pace of a trotting horse. Hylaeosaurus had weak jaws and small teeth. It would spend its time eating ground plants and large insects. Dinosaurs of the ankylosaur families account for one in ten of all dinosaur remains.

Length: 20 feet
Weight: 2 tons
Lived: Early Cretaceous
Found: England

Hypselosaurus
(HIP-sih-luh-sawr-us)

This is one of the lesser known members of the sauropod ("lizard foot") dinosaurs within the family of titanosaurids, or "giant lizards." It was a distant relative of the big plant eaters like *Diplodocus* and *Apatosaurus*. The members of the "giant lizard" family each had a steep, sloping head set on a short neck. Their teeth were peg-shaped and their mouths were small. These dinosaurs also had long, slim tails. Hypselosaurus means "high ridge lizard," and this dinosaur was called so because it had a particularly high back. At 40 feet long, it was a relatively small member of the family. Other members of the family were up to 70 feet long.

Scientists have discovered eggs from Hypselosaurus that may be the biggest of all dinosaur eggs. Each egg is 12 inches long and 10 inches in diameter. It could contain almost 6 pints of liquid. The surface of each egg is rough and pitted. Clusters of five eggs have been found in nests. They are the only eggs positively known to come from a specific dinosaur.

Length: 40 feet
Weight: 30–40 tons
Lived: Late Cretaceous
Found: France, Spain

Hypsilophodon
(hip-sih-LO-fuh-don)

This particular dinosaur survived for more than 100 million years. It first appeared at the end of the early Jurassic period and lived until all the dinosaurs died out 65 million years ago. Hypsilophodon belonged to the same family as *Dryosaurus*. It was smaller, perhaps only half the size of its larger relative. These were among the most fleet-footed dinosaurs ever. They could run fast and keep their balance at great speeds. They had horny beaks, and most had small upper teeth. Each foot had three toes and their small hands had five fingers.

Hypsilophodon had a special set of self-sharpening teeth in its cheeks. It may have had two rows of bony studs down the length of its back, and some of the studs may have continued onto the tail. Various skeletons show Hypsilophodon to have been between 4 feet, 6 inches and 7 feet, 6 inches long. Specimens have been found in England and Portugal as well as South Dakota. At least 20 partial skeletons have been unearthed.

Length: 6 feet, 7 inches
Weight: 130 pounds
Lived: Early Cretaceous
Found: United States (South Dakota), England, Portugal

Iguanodon
(ig-WAN-oh-don)

Named "iguana tooth" because it had teeth like modern iguana lizards, Iguanodon is one of the most famous dinosaurs. It belongs to a family similar to *Camptosaurus* but larger, heavier, and better equipped to eat. Its mouth was large, with teeth in the cheeks. In front was a bony beak like *Hypsilophodon*. Iguanodon usually stood on all fours. It had big, strong thighs and three-toed feet. Its smaller front legs each had four fingers and a spiked thumb. When it reared up to rest on the base of its tail, it would have stretched up to 16 feet tall. It had a length of almost 30 feet.

Iguanodon first appeared more than 120 million years ago and lived 55 million years, becoming extinct at the same time as all the other dinosaurs. Other members of the Iguanodon family included *Muttaburrasaurus* and *Ouranosaurus*. Iguanodon probably roamed swampy countryside, wading through hot marshland looking for food. It could wrap its long tongue around reeds and thick grasses. Sucked into its large mouth, small branches and tough roots would be crunched with its two rows of cheek teeth.

Length: 29 feet
Weight: 5 tons
Lived: Early Cretaceous
Found: Europe, Romania, North America, North Africa, Mongolia

Indosuchus
(in-doe-SOOK-us)

This dinosaur was named Indosuchus, or "Indian crocodile," because it was found in India. Its name is misleading, since the animal has nothing at all to do with crocodiles! Only a few bone fragments have been found, but they indicate that Indosuchus belonged to the great family of tyrannosaurids. The most famous member of this family was *Tyrannosaurus*. The fragments available show that Indosuchus was smaller than its more fearsome cousin. It had more teeth, but they were shorter and less effective. It also seems to have weighed less for its size.

Members of the tyrannosaurid family have been found all over the world. Among these are *Albertosaurus*, *Daspletosaurus*, *Labocania*, and *Tarbosaurus*. In addition to India, they have also been found in Asia, Russia, North America, and South America. These giant carnivors populated much of the earth by the end of the Cretaceous period. They developed over a long period of time and must have adapted slowly to survive as well as they did. Indosuchus probably looked like a more primitive and older relative of *Tyrannosaurus*.

Length: 30 feet
Weight: 4 tons
Lived: Late Cretaceous
Found: India

Ingenia
(in-JEN-ee-ah)

Oviraptorids, or "egg thieves," was a family with two members. One was called Ingenia, which means "genius." The other, which gave its name to the family, was called *Oviraptor*. Both belonged to a very large group of separate, closely linked families. The group members were called coelurosaurs, or "hollow tailed-lizards," because they all had thin, fragile bones, long legs, and shorter arms. Other important families included *Avimimus*, *Compsognathus*, *Ornithomimus*, *Dromaeosaurus*, and *Stenonychosaurus*. In all, 60 different types of dinosaurs in 14 families made up this group.

Ingenia was discovered in 1981 and had thicker fingers than *Oviraptor*. Of three fingers on each hand, the first was longest, followed by the second. Each finger had a curved claw. At about 6 feet long, Ingenia was a little smaller than *Oviraptor*. It was found in southwest Mongolia, and it is likely that others lived elsewhere in Asia.

Length: 6 feet
Weight: 60 pounds
Lived: Late Cretaceous
Found: Mongolia

Kentrosaurus
(KEN-truh-sawr-us)

One of the stegosaurid, or "plated dinosaur," family, Kentrosaurus means "pointed lizard." It was named for the spines on its back. Other members of this family included *Dacentrurus*, *Stegosaurus*, and *Tuojiangosaurus*. All these dinosaurs walked on four legs and had very tough skins. Kentrosaurus had pairs of short, triangular shaped plates on its neck and shoulders. Halfway along its back, the plates were replaced with long spikes. The spikes were set in pairs along the back and the tail. An extra spike grew from the top of each thigh.

Plated dinosaurs changed from their first appearance in the middle of the Jurassic period 160 million years ago. Various members of the family appeared at different times. Kentrosaurus was known to exist as far back as the late Jurassic, about 150 million years ago. Compared with giants like *Stegosaurus*, Kentrosaurus was quite small. It was little more than half the size of its larger relative.

Length: 17 feet
Weight: 1 ton
Lived: Late Jurassic
Found: Tanzania

Kritosaurus
(KRIT-uh-sawr-us)

Some scientists think this dinosaur was a very close relative of *Hadrosaurus*. It had a flat, broad head and a humped nose. It belonged to the duckbill family and lived toward the end of the dinosaur age. Kritosaurus means "noble lizard." Its humped nose reminded some people of the nose of a noble Roman senator!

Remains of Kritosaurus have been dug up in New Mexico and Baja California. Skeletons show it to have been about 30 feet long and up to 15 feet tall. It probably weighed nearly 3 tons. Duckbill dinosaurs had webbed feet and could probably swim. They would only do this to escape predators. Most of them lived in forests and woods.

Female Kritosaurus laid eggs in nests and stayed to look after them. Most male dinosaurs roamed away from the nest while females nursed the eggs until they hatched. Then they tended the young until they had grown up.

Length: 30 feet
Weight: 3 tons
Lived: Late Cretaceous
Found: United States (New Mexico), Mexico (Baja California)

45

Labocania
(lab-o-KAY-nee-uh)

A relative of *Tyrannosaurus* and *Megalosaurus*, this Cretaceous dinosaur was a fearsome flesh eater. It was much smaller than *Tyrannosaurus* and has not yet been attached to a known dinosaur family. It probably belonged to a group of more than 15 similar dinosaurs. Labocania had a much bigger head than *Tyrannosaurus* and a much bigger body. In many other ways it was very similar to its bigger relative. With enormous teeth and sharp claws on its toes, Labocania would have been a frightening predator. Yet its weight, which averaged about 3 tons, probably slowed it down and allowed it to be attacked by other flesh eaters. Some scientists think it had a very thick skin, which would have made it tough to kill. Only a few bones of Labocania have ever been found. They were dug up in the La Bocana Roja rock formations in Baja California.

Length: 25 feet
Weight: 3 tons
Lived: Late Cretaceous
Found: Mexico (Baja California)

Lambeosaurus
(LAM-be-uh-sawr-us)

A member of the duckbill family, Lambeosaurus was named after Lawrence Lambe, a Canadian scientist who spent much of his life studying dinosaurs. Literally the word means "Lambe's lizard." There were two types of duckbills. One group had head crests made of hollow bone, and the other group did not. Lambeosaurus was a member of the crested group and was the largest crested type known. Remains have been found in western North America, from Canada to Baja California.

With a very large tail and an enormous crest, Lambeosaurus was a monster, almost four stories tall on his back legs. Some skulls have been found with a crest bigger than the head. Others look like they might have had a small neck frill made of bone. One type had a very deep tail, which would have made it a good swimmer. This would be unusual, since it is not thought dinosaurs were happy in water. Rock impressions of its pebbly skin show Lambeosaurus to have had a leathery hide. Lambeosaurus is known to have lived about 85 million years ago.

Length: 49 feet
Weight: 2 tons
Lived: Late Cretaceous
Found: Mexico (Baja California), United States (Montana), Canada (Alberta)

Lesothosaurus
(leh-SOTH-uh-sawr-us)

Named after Lesotho, the country in Africa where it was first discovered, Lesothosaurus was a very close relative of *Fabrosaurus*. It was a member of the "bird-footed" (ornithopod) family. Built for browsing and running away if attacked, the back legs were strong and had three main claws on each foot. In addition, each foot had a small claw higher up the shin. Each tiny hand had four main fingers and a tiny, stub-like thumb. Like *Fabrosaurus*, Lesothosaurus was only 3 feet long and lived in the late Triassic, more than 200 million years ago. Unlike its close relative, it had narrower teeth. Its front teeth were smooth and pointed. Some scientists say the cheek teeth look like serrated arrow heads.

Small dinosaurs of this family are thought by some to have been the ancestors of almost all the "bird-foot" dinosaurs. No larger than a big dog, they survived at least 70 million years before dying out. Eventually, long before they vanished, other more powerful "bird-hips" had arrived.

Length: 3 feet, 4 inches
Weight: 40 pounds
Lived: Late Triassic/Early Jurassic
Found: South Africa

Lexovisaurus
(lex-OH-vuh-sawr-us)

This dinosaur is one of the oldest relatives of *Stegosaurus* known to have been found anywhere. It was very similar to *Kentrosaurus* but lived several million years earlier. It was discovered in remains found around the town of Lyon in France. An ancient Gallic people called Lexovi once lived in the area. Because of this, scientists called it Lexovisaurus ("Lexovi lizard"). Other bones were found in other parts of France, and fossil remains were also discovered in England. Those found in England are for an animal about the same size as *Kentrosaurus*. Some scientists think they have found more remains that suggest some members of the same family were much larger.

With more varied plates and spikes than *Kentrosaurus*, Lexovisaurus had narrow plates on its back and spines on its tail. Like its descendent, it had large spikes protecting each thigh. It is likely that dinosaurs of this type roamed across large areas of the earth. Several members of the same family would cross the same paths many times. More than 4,000 miles separate England from Tanzania, where *Kentrosaurus* was found!

Scientists are not sure why Lexovisaurus, and other members of its family, had bony plates along its back. Some people think it was for protection, although the animal would have been exposed along the sides of its body. Others believe it helped the animal radiate heat and keep its body temperature comfortable.

Length: 17 feet
Weight: 1 ton
Lived: Mid Jurassic
Found: England, France

Lufengosaurus
(loo-FEN-guh-sawr-us)

Distantly related to *Anchisaurus*, but larger, heavier, and stronger, Lufengosaurus belonged to the "flat lizard" (plateosaurid) family. It is known to have appeared about 210 million years ago. This member of the plateosaurid family was found in Lu-feng, making it the oldest dinosaur from China. It had strong jaws and short, widely spaced teeth. Because of this, scientists think it ate small animals as well as munching plants and small trees. Lufengosaurus probably walked on all fours. To get food they could rear up on their hind legs, using their long, strong tails for balance.

For a while, Lufengosaurus and its family relatives may have dominated large parts of the earth. It was the time when dinosaurs were just beginning to appear. Another famous relative, which gave its name to the entire family, is *Plateosaurus*. Different family members have been dug up in North America, Europe, and Africa. They are not thought to have lived long. They probably died out by the early Jurassic period.

Length: 20 feet
Weight: 1,800 pounds
Lived: Late Triassic/Early Jurassic
Found: China

Maiasaura
(mah-ee-ah-SAWR-uh)

Maiasaura is called "good mother lizard" because it was found with nests and babies. It belonged to the group of duckbill dinosaurs. Other members of the same family were *Edmontosaurus* and *Hadrosaurus*. They had flat heads without crests and a long, straight bottom jaw. They would browse among trees and long grasses munching food as they slowly ambled along. Maiasaura was dug up in Montana and had a bony spike growing from the top of its head. This dinosaur was discovered in 1978. With it were several nests, each one 7 feet across and more than 2 feet deep. Each nest was in the form of a mound. The eggs, shaped like sausages, were set out in the mound like spokes in a wheel. Each layer of eggs was separated with a layer of sand. The top layer was completely covered over. The young were found near the nest. This suggests that when they hatched they stayed close to home. These newly hatched Maiasaura were about 18 inches long and had badly worn teeth. The mother probably brought them food.

Length: 30 feet
Weight: 1 ton
Lived: Late Cretaceous
Found: United States (Montana)

Mamenchisaurus
(mah-MEN-chee-sawr-us)

This unusual dinosaur was a close relative of *Diplodocus* and *Apatosaurus*. Dinosaurs in this family were unusually long. Mamenchisaurus was discovered in south-central China and named from the area in which it was found – Mamenchi. From its bones, scientists guess that it was about 72 feet long, with the longest neck of any dinosaur yet discovered. In fact, its neck was so long it contained 19 neck bones, called vertebrae. From its "shoulders" to its head, Mamenchisaurus measured 33 feet!

Some of the vertebrae had struts to help stiffen the neck. Some scientists believe it may have developed this neck to reach very high branches of tall trees. Others believe it spent most of its life in rivers and ponds, sweeping its neck around to feed from the bank. This is not very likely. It probably combed leaves from twigs on trees. It may even have reared up to rest on the base of its spine. If it did, it could have reached leaves 50 feet above the ground.

Length: 72 feet
Weight: 10 tons
Lived: Late Jurassic
Found: China (Mamenchi)

Massospondylus
(mass-o-SPON-dih-lus)

Massospondylus was a close relative of *Lufengosaurus* and *Plateosaurus*, and a distant relative of *Thecodontosaurus*, and its name means "bulky spine bone." In most aspects it was similar to its close relatives, except that it was smaller. Dinosaurs of this type were common over 200 million years ago, during the late Triassic and early Jurassic periods. Fossil remains of Massospondylus were found in southern Africa. Bones similar to this type have also been found as far away as India.

Massospondylus had much larger hands than any of its relatives. In each thumb was a large, curved claw. This may have been a defensive weapon, but it is more likely that the claw was used to increase its diet. Instead of munching plants and small animals, it could dig up juicy roots and tear out small trees. This dinosaur had stones and pebbles in its stomach to grind up food. Its primitive teeth were not capable of tearing up plant food in its mouth.

Length: 13 feet
Weight: 1,200 pounds
Lived: Late Triassic/Early Jurassic
Found: South Africa

Megalosaurus
(MEG-uh-lo-sawr-us)

This was the very first dinosaur to be named. It was identified in 1824 and called "big lizard" because it was so large. At that time people thought it was just another old reptile. They did not know it belonged to a completely different group of animals that lived many millions of years ago. Described by Oxford University Professor Robert Plot in 1677, the thigh bone of Megalosaurus was said to come from a giant man! Nearly 150 years later it was identified as belonging to a relative of *Allosaurus*. Megalosaurus belonged to a family of at least 17 different types of flesh-eating dinosaurs.

It was a big, heavy predator distantly related to that terrifying meat eater, *Tyrannosaurus*. Megalosaurus had curved teeth with a saw-tooth edge and strong claws on each toe and finger. By studying footprints of this beast found all over Europe, South America, Africa, and Asia, scientists guess that it waddled like a duck, its tail thrashing from side to side as it stumbled along. This is because its toes pointed inward.

Length: 30 feet
Weight: 1 ton
Lived: Early Jurassic to Early Cretaceous
Found: Europe, South America, Africa, Asia

Melanorosaurus
(mel-AN-or-uh-sawr-us)

Dinosaur hunters are unsure about Melanorosaurus. Some think it is the same animal as Euskelosaurus. Others identify it as very similar but different. Whatever it is called, it was a member of the "flat lizard" family named after *Plateosaurus*. These dinosaurs had broad hands and feet. Their legs probably stuck out sideways and they walked on all fours. Some, such as *Lufengosaurus*, could stand upright on their back legs. They all had blunt teeth and chewed plants and possibly small animals.

Melanorosaurus was the longest of the early dinosaurs and had legs like an elephant. Its bones were solid, like those of most dinosaurs of this period. Later, more advanced dinosaurs developed hollow bones to reduce their weight. This gave them greater agility. It allowed them to run and escape danger. They probably survived longer this way. With lighter bones came a better method of moving blood around the body.

Consequently, advanced dinosaurs were able to shed body heat as they ran. Long before that, though, Melanorosaurus was an important early dinosaur.

Scientists have thought a lot about how Melanosaurus and other similar dinosaurs moved around. Some think they were able to trot or run fast to escape danger. Others believe they were more like reptiles, unable to run fast and shed extra heat. Melanosaurus was certainly well developed, and although it appeared early in the age of dinosaurs it was more advanced than some that appeared later.

Length: 40 feet
Weight: 2 tons
Lived: Late Triassic/Early Jurassic
Found: South Africa

Microceratops
(my-kro-SAIR-uh-tops)

Literally named "little horned face," this tiny plant eater is one of the smallest dinosaurs yet discovered. Fully grown, an adult would stretch little more than 2 feet long from beak to tail. It belonged to the family headed by *Protoceratops*. Its other well-known relative was *Bagaceratops*. These were small, primitive, horned dinosaurs. Each had a differently shaped horn or bump on its face. Microceratops had a short neck frill made of bone. A horny beak helped it grovel among the undergrowth for food and a place to hide. Being so small, it would have made easy pickings for meat eaters.

Fossil bones found in Mongolia and east China show that Microceratops had longer back legs than its relatives. These legs were slender and strong enough to support its weight. Microceratops probably foraged on all fours. It would rear up and run on its back legs when startled. This little dinosaur was not around long and soon died out.

Length: 2 feet, 6 inches
Weight: 25 pounds
Lived: Late Cretaceous
Found: Mongolia

Microvenator
(my-kro-ven-AY-tor)

Microvenator is one of the smallest "hollow-tailed lizards" (coelurosaurs) discovered. Its name means "small hunter." This turkey-sized hunting dinosaur was dug up in Montana and lived in the early Cretaceous period. Its hollow bones made it lightweight. Microvenator stood only 30 inches tall, although its total length was almost 4 feet. It had a long neck with a small head. On its short arms were three fingers. Its long tail was built to help the dinosaur balance itself when standing up on its back legs.

Microvenator was related to *Coelurus*, *Ornitholestes*, and *Ornithomimoides*. These fast-moving, pecking little predators existed on earth for several million years. As a group, these families of dinosaurs survived for about 100 million years. All of them were descendents of the late Triassic *Coelophysis*. Although none could fly, they were the equal of pecking birds today. They would have cleaned up food left by larger animals.

Length: 2 feet, 6 inches
Weight: 14 pounds
Lived: Early Cretaceous
Found: United States (Montana), Tibet

Monoclonius
(mon-uh-CLO-nee-us)

This animal is one of the earliest horned dinosaurs to be discovered in western North America. It was called Monoclonius ("single stem") because it had a single horn on its nose and was a member of the family of horned dinosaurs called ceratopsians. There were two types of horned dinosaurs. One type, like Monoclonius, had short neck frills made of bone. The other type had longer frills. Other members of the short-frill type included *Brachyceratops*, *Centrosaurus*, *Pachyrhinosaurus*, and *Styrachosaurus*. The most famous relative was *Triceratops*, the biggest and the most feared.

Some people think *Brachyceratops* was a baby Monoclonius. *Brachyceratops* was about two-thirds the size of Monoclonius. Monoclonius was little more than half the size of *Triceratops*. Its head was large, about 6 feet long, and a single horn grew from the top of its nose. A small bump grew above each eye. The back edge of the neck frill had a row of bony knobs and two spikes that pointed forward. Monoclonius may have used its horn to topple small palm trees and its parrot-like beak to forage for juicy roots.

Length: 18 feet
Weight: 1 ton
Lived: Late Cretaceous
Found: Western North America

Muttaburrasaurus
(mut-tah-BUR-rah-sawr-us)

This large relative of *Iguanodon* was named after the place in Australia, called Muttaburra, where it was discovered. First named in 1981, it is one of the few dinosaurs to come from that country. Muttaburrasaurus has a close link with the *Camptosaurus* family. Many of its bones look more like *Camptosaurus* than *Iguanodon*. Because of that, some dinosaur scientists classify it with the *Camptosaurus* rather than the *Iguanodon* family. The differences between the two families are slight. Along with many others, they are all part of the "bird-foot" group called ornithopods. Muttaburrasaurus had a low head with a broad skull. Its mouth swept gently upward and it had teeth like garden shears. These sharp teeth would have helped it eat meat, although no one knows exactly what it did feed on. Like several dinosaurs, it probably ate meat as well as plants and roots. It had a spiked thumb on each hand, like *Iguanodon*, to help it forage or fend off attackers. Members of the *Iguanodon* family appeared at the beginning of the Cretaceous period, about 125 million years ago. Muttaburrasaurus dates from about 105 million years ago.

Length: 23 feet
Weight: 4 tons
Lived: Mid-Late Cretaceous
Found: Australia (Muttaburra)

Nemegtosaurus
(NEH-meh-tuh-sawr-us)

Skull bones found indicate that this dinosaur was a late member of the *Diplodocus* family. It has been named after Mongolia's Nemegt Basin where it was found. *Diplodocus* is not found in rocks from the late Cretaceous. The skull named Nemegtosaurus is very similar to a *Diplodocus* skull. It has the same sloping shape. Other Nemegtosaurus bones have also been found. It may be that *Diplodocus* lived in this later period also, but that no bones have yet been found in rocks that date from this time. Nemegtosaurus was probably as long as *Diplodocus*, with a slender body, long neck, and long tail.

Nemegtosaurus is related to *Mamenchisaurus*. It does not, however, have that dinosaur's extremely long neck. Other members of the family came from the late Jurassic, about 50 million years before Nemegtosaurus roamed these hidden places deep in Asia. It is possible that isolated groups of dinosaurs lived on for millions of years after their relatives had died out. The headless skeleton of another dinosaur was found with Nemegtosaurus. Some scientists believe it was part of the same animal.

Length: 87 feet
Weight: 12 tons
Lived: Late Cretaceous
Found: Mongolia (Nemegt Basin)

Nodosaurus
(no-doe-SAWR-us)

This medium-sized armored dinosaur has been found all over North America, from New Jersey to Wyoming. It had rows of large and small plates down its back and its sides, or flanks. Its skin had bony buttons, called nodes, between its ribs. Small spikes were attached to the plates. It would have been a tough beast to eat! None of these bony plates and spikes were attached to its skeleton. For this reason, dinosaur scientists are not exactly sure where they were positioned.

In some families of armored dinosaurs, each member had a bony club at the end of its tail. Nodosaurus belonged to a group that had no club. Instead, its tail just trailed along the ground as its low head foraged for food. Node dinosaurs have been found in many countries, including France, Spain, England, India, China, and Australia. The largest members of the family were about 25 feet long and weighed more than 3 tons.

Length: 18 feet
Weight: 2—3 tons
Lived: Late Cretaceous
Found: United States (Kansas, Wyoming, New Jersey)

Opisthocoelicaudia
(o-piss-tho-SEE-luh-caw-dee-uh)

When Polish scientists were looking for dinosaurs in the Gobi Desert of Mongolia, they found remains of this animal without its neck bones or a skull. They called it the "backward hollow-tail dinosaur." It had four legs of almost equal length, and its tail was held high. Rigid bone links kept the tail level but about 5 feet off the ground. When they looked further, the scientists found a skull that they called *Nemegtosaurus*. Some experts think the two are the same animal. Others say the head does not match the skeleton found several miles away.

Opisthocoelicaudia may have sat back on the base of its tail. With its front legs and neck up in the air it could have reached very high trees and branches to feed off leaves. Scientists say the bones of this dinosaur are similar to the bones of freshwater turtles. Some turtles prop themselves up on the base of their tails. Some turtles curl their tails round big stones to anchor themselves. The dinosaur may have done this also.

Length: 40 feet
Weight: 15 tons
Lived: Late Cretaceous
Found: Mongolia (Gobi Desert)

Ornitholestes
(or-nith-o-LESS-teez)

A lightly built meat eater, Ornitholestes was called "bird robber" because it was believed to chase primitive bird life. Scientists used to think it was the same as *Coelurus*, but they now see it as a different member of the same family. It had long and slim back legs with short front legs, or arms. With tough feet and a tiny claw on each of three toes, they were fast-running dinosaurs. Capable of dashing through undergrowth and across grassland, they may have preyed on the dead flesh of other dinosaurs. In this way they may have been the jackals of the dinosaur age, tearing up the flesh of dinosaurs killed by the great meat eaters like *Tyrannosaurus*.

With small hands, each supporting three fingers, they probably lived by rummaging and foraging. An almost complete skeleton of Ornitholestes was found in Wyoming. From this, scientists have pieced together a lot of information about the tiny predator. Lizards, frogs, and small mammals would have been easy prey for this fierce little hunter.

Length: 6 feet, 6 inches
Weight: 30 pounds
Lived: Late Jurassic
Found: United States (Wyoming)

Ornithomimus
(or-nith-uh-MY-mus)

Found widely in North America and Mongolia, this dinosaur was called "bird imitator" because it looked like an ostrich without feathers. As a member of the same family as *Dromiceiomimus*, *Elaphrosaurus*, *Gallimimus*, and *Struthiomimus*, Ornithomimus was lightly built with a delicate bone structure. It was basically all neck and tail, held together by a short, plump body. All members of this family had keen eyesight, were quick, and could leap about at great speed.

Ornithomimus had a long mouth with no teeth and a small head. It had a large brain and was not stupid. There were three toes on each foot and three fingers on each hand. Its arms were so small they were useless for real work and would have been good only for scratching the ground for things to eat. Feeding off insects, eggs, seeds, and small grubs, Ornithomimus would have little means of defending itself if attacked. This kept it alert for danger. With a top speed of around 35 MPH, Ornithomimus could outpace any other animal.

Length: 11 feet, 6 inches
Weight: 220 pounds
Lived: Late Cretaceous
Found: Western North America, Tibet

Othnielia
(oth-NEEL-ee-ah)

The bones of Othnielia were originally called Nanosaurus. They were discovered in 1877 by the fossil hunter Othniel Charles Marsh. Exactly one hundred years later they were renamed after the man who discovered them. The dinosaur was a small member of the "bird-foot" family named after *Hypsilophodon*. It was much older than others in the same family, such as *Parkosaurus*. Othnielia was very like *Hypsilophodon*, except it had hardened enamel on both sides of its teeth. Its jaws were built to chop plants and chew them up before swallowing. The tip of the pointed mouth had a small beak-like pincer. Its jaws had strong muscles to cope with tough food. It also had an unusual hinge in the back of its mouth. When its upper and lower jaws came together, they swiveled around so both sets of teeth met exactly together.

Like others in the family, Othnielia had three toes on each foot and fingers on each hand. These dinosaurs were among some of the most successful at surviving. They lived about 100 million years before they died out.

Length: 4 feet, 6 inches
Weight: 50 pounds
Lived: Late Jurassic
Found: Western North America

Ouranosaurus
(our-AHN-uh-sawr-us)

One of the strangest dinosaurs, Ouranosaurus was discovered from remains found in West Africa. It belonged to the family of *Iguanodons* and was close in size to *Muttaburrasaurus*. It was a typical duckbill, with a flat head and an upturned mouth. It would often drop down on all fours but could also stand up on its back legs. Members of the *Iguanodon* family have been found all over the world. They stayed on earth for a long time, and Ouranosaurus may have been an ancestor of the duck-billed dinosaurs that appeared in the late Cretaceous period.

One other feature set Ouranosaurus apart from its relatives. It had a thin sail made of skin running from the back of its neck to the end of its tail. There may also have been a piece of skin under its chin. The skin probably carried blood vessels. These would remove heat from the body of the dinosaur. The heat would be carried to the surface of the skin and radiated away into the air. In this way the dinosaur would cool itself in hot weather. In cold conditions, the sail would have gathered heat from the sun. The blood would have carried heat to the body, arms, and legs to warm them.

Length: 23 feet
Weight: 4 tons
Lived: Early Cretaceous
Found: West Africa

59

Oviraptor
(o-vee-RAP-tor)

The first skeleton of this dinosaur was found in 1923, close to a nest of *Protoceratops* eggs. Because of this, scientists thought it was an "egg thief," which Oviraptor means in Latin. It had a short head and a deep, short beak that curved downward. Its skull looks like the skull of a flamingo, but there is no link between the two. Oviraptor has only one close relative, *Ingenia*. They are both members of the "hollow-tailed lizard" group. They probably descended from the family of *Ornithomimus* and its relatives. Oviraptor has much larger fingers and bigger claws than *Ingenia*. It also has three toes on each foot, with a small "big toe" that is practically useless. Each large toe had a claw attached. Both *Ingenia* and Oviraptor come from Mongolia.

Oviraptor may have had some feathers on its body, but it could not fly. It was probably a scavenger, tearing up the leftovers from big meat eaters like *Tyrannosaurus*.

Length: 6 feet
Weight: 60 pounds
Lived: Late Cretaceous
Found: Mongolia

Pachycephalosaurus
(pak-ee-SEF-uh-lo-sawr-us)

This dinosaur was a very large member of the "bonehead" family. All members of the family had thick skulls. Some had a thick knob on top of the skull that looked like a crash helmet. Some of these animals were quite small, less than 3 feet in size. A relative, *Homalocephale*, was 10 feet long. Pachycephalosaurus was the biggest of the boneheads and towered above its relatives. It also had the thickest skull, with which it could charge its enemies and knock them senseless. There was only one problem with a thick skull. It left little room for brains!

Scientists have carefully measured the skull of different boneheads and found that Pachycephalosaurus had a dense cap of bone 10 inches thick. It had some small, bony spikes jutting up from its nose and sharp knobs around the back of its head. Charging at full speed, it would have made a terrific impact. It may also have used its head to ram others in its family. Some animals do this today to claim territory or to warn off others. Pachycephalosaurus lived in North America, but others in the large family have been found all over the world.

Length: 15 feet
Weight: 450 pounds
Lived: Late Cretaceous
Found: Western North America

Pachyrhinosaurus
(PAK-ee-rye-no-sawr-us)

Bone hunters in Alberta dug up the fossil remains of a very unusual member of the "horned dinosaur" family. The most familiar member of this family was *Triceratops*. Others included *Centrosaurus*, *Eoceratops*, *Monoclonius*, and *Styracosaurus*. Each had one or more horns on its face. Pachyrhinosaurus had no horn but had a squat stump on the top of its nose. The stump, shaped like a plate, was 22 inches long and 14 inches wide. The bone was 5 inches deep with a volcano-shaped crater in the middle. Bone knobs had grown above the eyes.

All horned dinosaurs had either a short frill or a large frill. Pachyrhinosaurus belonged to the short-frilled family. It had short spikes of bone growing from the back of the frill. Like all horned dinosaurs, it had a parrot-like beak with which it groveled for food. The stump on the nose of this dinosaur might have been used to ram other animals or to knock small trees down by charging them with its head.

Length: 18 feet
Weight: 1 ton
Lived: Late Cretaceous
Found: Canada (Alberta)

Palaeoscincus

(pay-lee-o-SKINK-us)

Known only by a single tooth and some odd bones found in Montana, this dinosaur is a member of the "node lizard" family. Some scientists have said it is the same as *Panoplosaurus*, but most agree it is different. Node lizards (called nodosaurids) were very heavily armored, four-footed dinosaurs. They are known to have lived throughout North America, Europe, and Asia. They probably descended from *Hylaeosaurus* about 125 million years ago. Some scientists think *Hylaeosaurus* was descended from *Scelidosaurus*.

Palaeoscincus was larger than some other node lizards. Scientists believe there were about 19 different types. Some were only 7 feet long. Others were up to 25 feet in length. They walked well above the ground but their heads were low. The neck was short and allowed little movement. Safe inside their bony armor, they would have been troubled by few dinosaurs.

Length: 23 feet
Weight: 3 tons
Lived: Late Cretaceous
Found: United States (Montana)

Panoplosaurus

(pan-OP-luh-sawr-us)

Because of its bony plates and protective spikes, this dinosaur was called "fully armored lizard." It was one of the last armored dinosaurs from North America. Its back was protected by hard plates made of bone. Large slabs of bone were attached to its skull. These protected its neck and the sides of its head. Its skin was covered with bony lumps set in the thick skin.

Panoplosaurus had a massive head. It was arched on top and had a narrow snout. This too was covered with bony plates. In its mouth, Panoplosaurus had small teeth with ridges. From the teeth, scientists believe it fed on roots and dug out small bush plants. Dinosaurs like Panoplosaurus were very heavily defended and protected with bony armor. Yet they had weak jaws and poor teeth. They would have spent a lot of time gathering up food with their bony snouts. Protected from attack inside their bony plates and a skin several inches thick, they were little more than eating machines.

Length: 23 feet
Weight: 3 tons
Lived: Late Cretaceous
Found: Western North America

Parasaurolophus

(par-ah-sawr-OL-uh-fus)

A large member of the duckbill family of dinosaurs, called hadrosaurids, Parasaurolophus was a close relative of *Lambeosaurus*. Most duckbills were divided into two groups. One had a flat head with no crest. The second group had tall, bony head crests. Each family had a different crest style and families would recognize each other this way. Parasaurolophus had a very special crest. It was a curved, hollow horn that attached to the front of the head and swept backwards.

The horn was more than 6 feet long. Inside, two tubes went up to the top and two came back down. These were breathing tubes. Each pair of tubes going up into the crest was attached to the nostrils in the dinosaur's nose. The down tubes went to the lungs. Scientists have measured the tubes. They believe Parasaurolophus could make a very loud bellowing sound by snorting through these sound tubes.

Length: 33 feet
Weight: 2 tons
Lived: Late Cretaceous
Found: United States (Utah, New Mexico), Canada (Alberta)

Parksosaurus
(PARKS-uh-sawr-us)

When this dinosaur was discovered, lying on its side in an Alberta fossil field, it was known to be a close relative of *Hypsilophodon*. It was named after the man who found it, Canadian bone hunter W.A. Parks. Members of the *Hypsilophodon* family were all between 3 feet and 10 feet long. They developed early in the dinosaur age and lived for more than 100 million years. Parksosaurus and its relatives belonged to the "bird foot" dinosaurs. Bird foots were able to stand up and run on their back legs and included a wide range of dinosaur families. *Hypsilophodon* and its very close relatives appeared around the late Jurassic or early Cretaceous. Parksosaurus came much later and dates from the late Cretaceous. Larger and heavier than *Hypsilophodon*, Parksosaurus had a long neck and a small head. Its teeth were different from those of other dinosaurs in its family. Its other features, though, made it very similar to its relatives.

Length: 8 feet
Weight: 150 pounds
Lived: Late Cretaceous
Found: Canada (Alberta)

Parrosaurus
(PAR-uh-sawr-us)

This dinosaur belonged to the "lizard foot" family of sauropods. It was probably similar to *Baraposaurus*, but it may have been smaller. It was named after Albert Parr, the American animal scientist. Only a few back bones have been found. From these, it has been possible to build a picture of what it must have looked like.

Parrosaurus belongs to the late Cretaceous, the period just before the time all the dinosaurs died out. It was probably a descendent of *Camarasaurus*. Like all members of the sauropod group, it had a long neck and a small head. Although its brain was very small compared to the size of its body, it was not stupid.

Parrosaurus was a plant eater and would have spent a lot of time nibbling leaves and chewing up its food. With a body the size of a bus, it took a lot of time to fill its stomach!

Some people think Parrosaurus would have reared up on its back legs to reach tall branches and extra food. To support themselves in that position, these dinosaurs probably sat on the base of their tail.

Length: 40 feet
Weight: 30 tons
Lived: Late Cretaceous
Found: United States (Carolinas, Missouri)

Pentaceratops
(PEN-tah-sair-uh-tops)

Pentaceratops means "five horned face." This dinosaur had a short horn on its nose, two large horns above its eyebrows, and a bony stub on each cheek. It was a member of the long-frilled group of horned dinosaurs. Pentaceratops appeared about 75 million years ago. This was about 5 million years after one of its ancestors, *Chasmosaurus*. In turn, it was an ancestor of *Torosaurus*. Pentaceratops had more horns than any other horned dinosaur. Its neck frill was very long, with knobs on the back edge.

Pentaceratops had one of the largest frills of any long-frilled dinosaur. Its head was 7 feet, 6 inches long, more than one third its entire length. Holes in the bone structure of the frill reduced its weight. Large and powerful muscles were anchored to the frill, helping it work its beak-like mouth to good effect. Bones from this dinosaur have been found in New Mexico. It was one in a long line of gradually changing members of the horned dinosaur group.

Length: 20 feet
Weight: 2 tons
Lived: Late Cretaceous
Found: United States (New Mexico), Canada (Alberta)

Pinacosaurus
(pin-AH-kuh-sawr-us)

Plateosaurus
(PLAY-tee-uh-sawr-us)

This was the most common of the early dinosaurs known to science. Plateosaurus means "flat lizard," and it has given its name to a family of at least seven different types. Others include *Lufengosaurus* and *Massospondylus*. Plateosaurus was larger than either of these. It had a very thick tail with strong muscles. It would have been able to use the base of its spine as a prop. By doing this and rearing up on its hind legs, it could tear down branches of high trees or munch the tops of palms.

These dinosaurs date from the end of the Triassic, more than 200 million years ago. They and their relatives have been found all over the world. Plateosaurus must have been particularly common in Europe, where many fossil bones have been found. These dinosaurs lived for many millions of years before they died out. Some scientists think that they were the true ancestors of the giant, four-footed sauropods like *Apatosaurus* and *Diplodocus*.

This dinosaur was called "plank lizard" because it had a heavily armored back. It was a member of the "fused lizard" group, which also included *Ankylosaurus*, *Euoplocephalus*, and *Sauroplites*. It had a broad mouth and a beak-like face. Its legs were directly below its body and held it off the ground. All members of this family had a big bone club at the end of a long tail. Pinacosaurus had sharp spikes along its back and sides. Bones from this dinosaur have been found in China and Mongolia.

Pinacosaurus was one of the smallest in the "fused lizard" group. It was only half the size of the massive *Ankylosaurus*. It lived in hot, dry climates high above sea level. Food might have been difficult to find where it lived, but it probably went around without challenge. Not many dinosaurs liked very hot places.

Length: 18 feet
Weight: 2 tons
Lived: Late Cretaceous
Found Mongolia, China

Length: 26 feet
Weight: 1 ton
Lived: Late Triassic
Found: Germany, France, Switzerland, England

Podokesaurus
(po-DOE-kee-sawr-us)

This little dinosaur may never have existed. Its name means "swift-footed lizard." Was Podokesaurus a separate animal or was it really a *Coelophysis?* It is known to have lived during the late Triassic or early Jurassic period. It belonged to the family of "hollow form" dinosaurs called coelophysids. Dinosaurs in that group were named after *Coelophysis*. They are known from the skeletons of many animals that lived and died together. It is believed they were all caught by a sudden sandstorm and buried alive. Many dinosaur scientists believe that Podokesaurus was a different animal, but very similar to *Coelophysis*. This little meat eater, alive at the dawn of the dinosaur age, would have stood only 2 feet tall. It was lightly built and had a long tail. It also had long hind legs and a pair of short arms with tiny hands. The bones of this little creature were found in Massachusetts, and no more have been found anywhere else.

Length: 10 feet
Weight: 65 pounds
Lived: Late Triassic
Found: Massachusetts

Procompsognathus
(pro-komp-so-NAY-thus)

This very small dinosaur was dug up in West Germany. It is one of the earliest, and most primitive of the family known as coelophysids, named after *Coelophysis*. It lived during the late Triassic and was the most distant ancestor of a large group of families called "hollow-tailed lizards," or coelurosaurs. In 1981, a dinosaur expert said that along with *Coelophysis*, Procompsognathus was so important it should be put in a special family of its own.

No longer than 4 feet, it was less than a foot tall at the hips. Its tiny skull was only 3 inches in length. Procompsognathus had long, thin legs and a long tail. Its arms were very short and each finger had tiny claws. These animals were fast runners and very successful. They may be thought of as the hyenas and roadrunners of the age of dinosaurs. Procompsognathus was the ancestor of a wide range of animals that lived all over North America, Europe, Africa, South America, and Asia. They ranged in size from dinosaurs the size of chickens to some the size of a small horse.

Length: 4 feet
Weight: 15 pounds
Lived: Late Triassic
Found: West Germany

Prosaurolophus
(pro-sawr-OL-uh-fus)

This dinosaur was the ancestor of *Saurolophus*. It had a sloping face with bumps over the eyebrows. Its mouth was flat and its lower jaw was straight. Prosaurolophus belonged to the family of duckbills that had flat heads or skulls. They did not have large crests or domes on their heads. Prosaurolophus did have a small bony lump that ended in a spike.

Compared to other duckbills, Prosaurolophus was not particularly large. Although some duckbills were only 12 feet long, others, like *Hadrosaurus*, were up to 32 feet in length. Prosaurolophus was 26 feet long, with a strong tail that it usually held straight out behind itself as it loped along on its hind legs. Prosaurolophus laid its eggs in mud mounds shaped like saucers. Some scientists think the adults gathered the young together to look after them. They may even have gathered food for them. Some had flaps of skin that could be blown up like balloons. They may have done this to make loud calls to others in the family.

Length: 26 feet
Weight: 1 ton
Lived: Late Cretaceous
Found: Canada (Alberta)

Protoceratops
(pro-toe-SAIR-uh-tops)

About the size of a pig, Protoceratops is the earliest known member of the family of horned dinosaurs. Its name means "first horned face." Many skeletons were discovered by an American expedition to Mongolia in 1922. This expedition also found nests with unhatched baby Protoceratops curled up inside eggs. The baby dinosaurs were only 12 inches long. The eggs were only 6 inches across and had been placed in rows around a bowl-shaped nest. The eggs were separated from each other by layers of sand. These were the first dinosaur eggs to be found.

The closest relatives to Protoceratops were *Bagaceratops* and *Microceratops*. Protoceratops had a large face and a small neck frill. It had a large beak and bumps on its nose and above its eyebrows. These bumps were the first signs of horns that would develop in later dinosaurs. Later horned dinosaurs like *Styracosaurus* and *Triceratops* had big horns and were much larger than Protoceratops.

Length: 6 feet
Weight: 1 ton
Lived: Late Cretaceous
Found: Mongolia

Psittacosaurus
(SIT-uh-ko-sawr-us)

This man-sized dinosaur is a member of the "parrot lizard" family. It is linked with the "horned face" dinosaurs. Psittacosaurus looked a bit like *Protoceratops* but had no bone neck frill. It had a beak like a parrot and a deep jaw. Its front legs were quite short, while its back legs were long and very strong. It probably ambled along on all fours and stood on its back legs to reach plants and branches.

Psittacosaurus had four toes on each foot, one of which was a stump like a short thumb. It had four fingers on each hand and claws on each finger and toe. These dinosaurs lived in the early and mid-Cretaceous period. They may have descended from the *Heterodontosaurus* family of the early Jurassic more than 90 million years earlier.

On one bone hunt, scientists found a baby Psittacosaurus only half the size of a pigeon. It is the smallest baby dinosaur found anywhere.

Length: 2 feet, 7 inches to 5 feet
Weight: Up to 50 pounds
Lived: Early Cretaceous
Found: Mongolia, China, USSR (Siberia)

Saichania
(sye-CHAY-nee-ah)

Some very good fossil bones of this dinosaur have been found in Mongolia. Its name, which means "beautiful one" in Mongolian, refers to the unusually good state of the fossils and not to the dinosaur's appearance!

Saichania belonged to the late Cretaceous family of armored dinosaurs (ankylosaurids). Members of the same family included *Ankylosaurus, Euoplocephalus, Pinacosaurus, Sauroplites,* and *Tarchia*. Saichania's size was about average for the armored dinosaurs, although much smaller than a huge *Ankylosaurus*.

Saichania had a larger skull than *Pinacosaurus*, with more bumpy bone on top. It had a large number of bone knobs, studs, and spikes in rows across its back and along its tail. Where the back legs were attached to its spine, separate bones were welded together for great strength. The bony club on the end of its tail was similar to the club on *Ankylosaurus*.

Length: 23 feet
Weight: 2 tons
Lived: Late Cretaceous
Found: Mongolia

Saltasaurus
(salt-uh-SAWR-us)

This relative of *Hypselosaurus* was a member of the "giant lizard" family. It is named after the Salta Province of Argentina, where it was found during the late 1970s. With a total length of 40 feet, Saltasaurus was one of the last of its kind to appear before all dinosaurs died out.

Scientists are very interested in Saltasaurus because it had armor plates all over its body. One of the large group of "lizard feet" (sauropod) dinosaurs, it is the first to have this protective cover. Each plate was between 2 inches and 4 inches in size. They were set in the skin, and each dinosaur probably had several thousand across its body.

Saltasaurus had a long tail with a very thick base. This allowed it to rest on the base of its tail and rear up to reach food high above ground. Like all sauropods, its head was small.

Length: 40 feet
Weight: 30 tons
Lived: Late Cretaceous
Found: Argentina

Saltopus
(SALT-o-pus)

This tiny dinosaur was a member of the "hollow tail" (coelurosaur) family. Because the scientist who discovered it thought it was a jumping dinosaur, he called it Saltopus, which means "leaping foot" in Latin. In fact, Saltopus was probably a fast runner. It is one of the oldest dinosaurs known and was found in a quarry in Scotland during a bone hunt in 1910. Scientists think it fed on small insects and lizards. It was closely related to *Coelophysis* and *Procompsognathus.*

Saltopus had small arms with five fingers on each hand. The fourth and fifth fingers were very small. It had strong muscles at the top of its back legs. These helped it move very fast over rough ground. Saltopus had a pointed face and mouth with rows of small teeth. It was only about the size of a domestic cat and stood 8 inches high at its hip.

Length: 2 feet
Weight: 2 pounds
Lived: Late Triassic
Found: Scotland

Saurolophus
(sawr-OL-o-fus)

Because it had a large piece of bone sticking out the back of its head, this dinosaur was given the Greek name for "crested lizard." It belonged to the group of "bird foot" dinosaurs and to the family of duckbills. It appeared just as *Corythosaurus* was dying out. It lived at the same times as *Lambeosaurus.* Examples of this dinosaur have been found in North America and Asia. It is a very advanced duckbill and is believed to date back only 75 million years.

Saurolophus looked a lot like *Edmontosaurus,* but it had a long head shaped like a spoon. The dinosaur probably stood 17 feet tall on its back legs and would have reached leaves and branches as high as the roof on a house. It had three hoofed toes on each foot and four webbed fingers on each hand. Two fingers on each hand were also hoofed. Its tail was big and flattened, with strong bones and muscles. This helped the animal control its balance as it shifted from four legs to two. Like all duckbills, it had no teeth in its beak. It did have sets of teeth in its cheeks.

Length: 30 feet
Weight: 1 ton
Lived: Late Cretaceous
Found: East Asia, North America

Sauroplites
(sawr-uh-PLY-teez)

This is one of the oldest of the "armored dinosaur" (ankylosaur) family and dates back to the early Cretaceous period. Its name means "stone-like lizard" and is taken from the name Hoplite, a heavily armored ancient Greek soldier. Its remains were found on the border between China and Mongolia.

Not many bones of Sauroplites have been found. Enough exist, however, to form a good picture of this early ankylosaur. It is smaller than *Saichania*, another member of the armored family which came much later.

Sauroplites was covered with bony segments set into its skin. It also had plates of bone in rows down its back and on its tail. Bony spikes were attached to the side of its body just behind the neck. These would have given it good protection from the flesh-eating dinosaurs of the Cretaceous period.

Length: 20 feet
Weight: 2 tons
Lived: Early Cretaceous
Found: China

Saurornithoides
(sawr-or-nith-OY-deez)

This small predator was more intelligent than most dinosaurs. Unlike other dinosaurs, its eyes could focus on one object. This allowed it to judge distance, a valuable asset when hunting. The large size of its eyes also enabled it to see well in poor light. Weight for weight, it had a brain six times larger than the brain of a crocodile!

Saurornithoides had a light bone structure and a long tail to help it balance on two legs. Its neck carried a long head with pointed face and small nostrils. In its mouth were small, sharp teeth with one edge serrated like the edge of a saw. It had relatively long arms and three long, grasping fingers on each hand. Each finger had a claw. On each foot were four toes, and one of the four toes had a claw that the dinosaur lifted off the ground when walking.

Because this dinosaur appeared in the late Cretaceous, it had the benefit of a long history evolving from many ancestors. Its name means "bird-like lizard" and it was closely related to *Stenonynchosaurus*.

Length: 6 feet, 6 inches
Weight: 70–90 pounds
Lived: Late Cretaceous
Found: Canada (southern Alberta)

Scelidosaurus
(skel-EE-doe-sawr-us)

This dinosaur was one of the early members of the armored groups that appeared in the early Jurassic period. It was quite similar to *Ankylosaurus* but appeared much earlier. It had a typical set of protective bone plates and knobs on its thick skin and a low-slung head.

Scelidosaurus means "rib lizard." This dinosaur has been found in places as far apart as England and Tibet. Impressions of its skin have been found by scientists and show a mass of tiny, rounded scales all over its body. It could have belonged to the family of *Stegosaurus* or *Ankylosaurus*. Scientists have not yet decided.

A lot of bones have been found that scientists have not yet fully examined. It is known, however, that Scelidosaurus was a primitive animal. It had badly developed teeth and would have moved slowly across the ground as it foraged for food. Nevertheless, it was well-protected from attack and would not have been an easy meal for early, flesh-eating predators.

Length: 11 feet, 6 inches
Weight: ?
Lived: Early Jurassic
Found: Southern England, Tibet

Scutellosaurus
(scoo-TEL-oh-sawr-us)

Tiny by comparison with other dinosaurs in existence at the time, Scutellosaurus was about the size of a fox, with long legs and a scaly back. It lived nearly 200 million years ago, right at the start of the age of dinosaurs. Scutellosaurus was only discovered in 1981, when bones were found in Arizona. It had a tail longer than the entire length of its body. It lived at the same time as *Fabrosaurus*, *Lesothosaurus*, and *Heterodontosaurus*.

This dinosaur is a close relative of *Lesothosaurus*. It had protective bony plates set in the skin on its back. Scutellosaurus had long back legs, but its front legs were quite short. Although it could probably run fast, Scutellosaurus would be no match for large flesh eaters like *Dilophosaurus*. It had a short head and ridged teeth. This would help it eat plants and small shrubs.

Length: 4 feet
Weight: 50 pounds
Lived: Early Jurassic
Found: United States (Arizona)

Segisaurus

(SEE-gih-sawr-us)

This very early member of the "hollow-tail lizard" family was probably a descendent of *Coelophysis*. It was about the size of a goose and was found in Arizona. Some scientists have likened it to *Procompsognathus*. However, both *Coelophysis* and *Procompsognathus* had hollow bones, while Segisaurus had solid bones.

Segisaurus was named after Segi Canyon, Arizona, where it was found in 1933. Unfortunately, only parts of the skeleton were found, without a head. This has made it very difficult to build up an accurate picture. The artist here has shown what scientists think its head might have looked like. The animal had long, slim back legs and feet very similar to *Procompsognathus*. These would have helped it run quite fast. Because the teeth have not been found, it is impossible to know precisely what it fed on. However, scientists believe it to have been interested in small lizards and tiny animals.

Remains of Segisaurus continue to puzzle scientists. The back-jutting hipbones have tiny holes in them, and the animal has a collarbone. The collarbone had almost disappeared in dinosaurs, even the early ones. Apart from its feet, there were other similarities between Segisaurus and *Procompsognathus*. The hipbones were almost identical, and the arm bones looked as though they belonged to the same family. Much of the work of comparing Segisaurus with *Procompsognathus* was carried out by Professor John Ostrom in 1981.

Length: 3 feet, 4 inches
Weight: 20 pounds
Lived: Early Jurassic
Found: United States (Arizona)

Shanshanosaurus
(shan-SHAN-uh-sawr-us)

This small dinosaur was found by fossil hunters in China. So far, this is the only specimen that has been discovered. The skeleton was built of very thin bones for light weight and flexibility. Its name is taken from the Shan-shan area of China, where it was found. A close relative, called *Noasaurus*, was found in Argentina. Each was like a cross between *Deinonychus* and *Dromaeosaurus*. *Noasaurus* had a terrifying claw on each foot like *Deinonychus*, but it was flexible and more sharply curved.

Shanshanosaurus had a large head shaped like a wedge. Its teeth were very sharp and its eyes were small. No doubt it had poor eyesight. It had a long neck, short arms, and long, muscular legs. On them, this fierce little predator could have moved fast across rough ground. It probably fed on small plant eaters or baby dinosaurs, such as the young of *Diplodocus* and *Apatosaurus*. Only big meat eaters like *Tyrannosaurus* could have gone after fully grown plant eaters. Dinosaurs like Shanshanosaurus probably had to make do with smaller animals.

Length: 6 feet
Weight: 25 pounds
Lived: Late Cretaceous
Found: China

Shantungosaurus
(shan-TUNG-o-sawr-us)

With a flat head and a huge body, Shantungosaurus is easily the biggest duckbill yet discovered. It turned up in Shantung, China, and belongs to the large family of hadrosaurine duckbills. It is closely related to *Edmontosaurus*, *Hadrosaurus*, *Maiasaura*, *Prosaurolophus*, and *Saurolophus*. Some members of the family may have been up to 50 feet long and stood 25 feet high. Shantungosaurus had a low skull with a flat top to its head, a flat beak, and no crest, as did some hadrosaurids.

Shantungosaurus was very similar to *Edmontosaurus* but much bigger. It dates from the late Cretaceous period and would have been an impressive sight. A full-scale reconstruction has been set up at the Natural History Museum in Beijing, the capital city of China. A full-grown man standing beside the reconstruction only comes up to the dinosaur's knee. Were it in existence today, Shantungosaurus would be looking over the tops of three-story houses!

Length: 39–49 feet
Weight: 3 tons
Lived: Late Cretaceous
Found: China

Silvisaurus
(SIL-vuh-sawr-us)

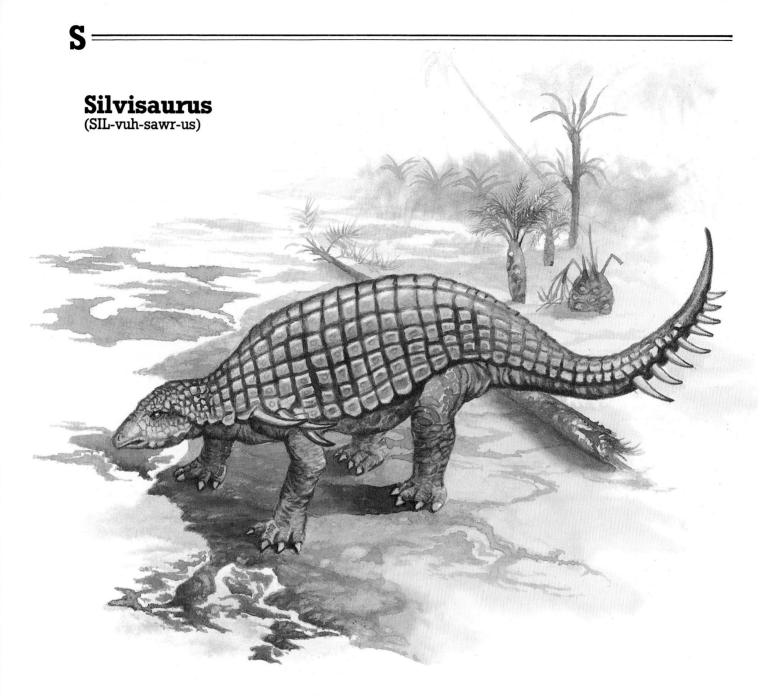

This dinosaur was first named in 1960 from bones dug up in Kansas. It was not complete, and the skeleton revealed only odd bones from the head, the neck, and some other parts of its body. These were enough to identify it, however. It belonged to the family of "node lizard" armored dinosaurs, called by scientists nodosaurid ankylosaurs. Other ankylosaurs were *Acanthopholis*, *Hoplitosaurus*, *Hylaeosaurus*, *Nodosaurus*, *Palaeoscincus*, and *Panoplosaurus*.

Scientists believe Silvisaurus to be a primitive member of the armored dinosaur family. It had a heavy head, a long neck, and a bulky body. It had several armor plates down its back and sides. Spikes covered its tail, but its tail did not end in a

bony club as some did. "Node lizards" look like their relatives, the "fused lizards," but lack the fused lizard's bony club at the end of the tail.

Length: 13 feet
Weight: 1 ton
Lived: Early Cretaceous
Found: United States (Kansas)

Spinosaurus
(SPY-nuh-sawr-us)

Several dinosaurs and other animals had large spines on their backs covered with skin. This gave these animals the appearance of having sails on their backs. *Ouranosaurus* was one. Spinosaurus is another. Both lived in the early Cretaceous. Spinosaurus was large and carried 6-foot spines on its back. Both *Ouranosaurus* and Spinosaurus were found from remains discovered in Africa. Skeletons of Spinosaurus also show it to have been a meat eater. It had teeth serrated like steak knives, but they were straight and not curved like those of some other dinosaurs.

Spinosaurus has been put in a group called spinosaurids. The group included several families, among them Altispinax. They were large carnivores and hunted widely for food and prey. The sail may have helped them warm up more quickly than other dinosaurs by taking in heat from the sun. This would have been an advantage when they set out hunting.

Length: 40 feet
Weight: 7 tons
Lived: Late Cretaceous
Found: Niger, Egypt

Staurikosaurus
(stor-IK-uh-sawr-us)

This dinosaur belongs in a family of its own. It has no known relatives. It is, however, part of a group of families known as prosauropods, or "before the lizard-feet dinosaurs." They included the first of the big, four-footed plant eaters like *Plateosaurus* as well as smaller, lighter animals like *Thecodontosaurus*.

Staurikosaurus was named after the Southern Cross, a group of stars best seen in the southern hemisphere. Staurikosaurus was found in southern Brazil. They were among the very first dinosaurs and are known to have existed more than 210 million years ago.

Dinosaurs of this family walked and ran on two legs but could have dropped to all fours if necessary. They had large heads, compact bodies, and sharp teeth. They had five fingers on each hand and five toes on each foot. The middle toes and fingers were the longest.

Length: 6 feet, 6 inches
Weight: Up to 66 pounds
Lived: Middle Triassic
Found: Brazil (Santa Maria)

Stegoceras
(steg-OSS-air-us)

This medium-sized "bonehead" dinosaur was a close relative of *Pachycephalosaurus*. It had a thick, smooth domed roof on the top of its skull. A frill of bony knobs grew around the back of the head just above the neck. Inside the skull, Stegoceras had a rather large brain. Its bone dome grew larger the older it got. The average skull thickness was about 3 inches, but males had thicker skulls than females. They may have used these in butting contests. All boneheads had spines that locked when they charged hard objects or other animals. This prevented severe damage when they collided.

Stegoceras was a plant eater like all dinosaurs in the group. They probably lived like goats live today and roamed high places where they would be safe from attack by flesh-eating dinosaurs. They seem to have been very widely distributed. Stegoceras has been found in places as far apart as North America and China.

Length: 6 feet, 6 inches
Weight: Up to 120 pounds
Lived: Late Cretaceous
Found: Western North America, China

Stegosaurus
(STEG-uh-sawr-us)

Stegosaurus was first discovered in 1877 from bones found in Colorado. Nobody really knows why it had such big, bony plates on its back. Some scientists think they were there to radiate excess heat from the animal's body. Others believe they were a protection from flesh-eating dinosaurs. Stegosaurus was closely related to *Kentrosaurus*, *Lexovisaurus*, and *Tuojiangosaurus*. Its name means "plated lizard" and refers to all the plates, spikes, and spines on its back and tail.

Stegosaurus had a very small, tube-like head, small teeth, and a brain the size of a walnut. Nevertheless, it could defend itself by lashes from armored spikes on its tail. Its front legs were only half the length of its back legs. The dinosaur probably munched small plants and tree roots, nibbling leaves from small trees or foliage from bushes. Many Stegosaurus bones have been found in Oklahoma, Utah, and Wyoming. Others have turned up in Europe, Africa, India, and China.

Length: 30 feet
Weight: 2 tons
Lived: Late Jurassic
Found: United States (Colorado, Wyoming, Oklahoma, Utah)

Stenonychosaurus
(sten-ON-ik-uh-sawr-us)

If brain size is an indication of intelligence, Stenonychosaurus must have been one of the most intelligent dinosaurs to exist. With a large brain and huge eyes, it was very similar to *Saurornithoides*, its relative. In other ways, it was like the family of *Dromaeosaurus*. It had a long, stiffened tail, long arms, a second toe with a claw, and strong back legs. It also had wide-set eyes for good focusing. It would have judged distance well. Clearly, Stenonychosaurus was agile, quick-moving, and quick-thinking. It probably stalked its prey like many animals do today. Most dinosaurs survived by instinct. Stenonychosaurus could get the better of its prey by using brain power to respond to its developed senses. These included sight, sound, and smell. It probably had fast reflexes and could dart about at great speed. Fossil remains have been found in Canada, and they date back about 80 million years.

Length: 6 feet, 6 inches
Weight: 60 to 100 pounds
Lived: Late Cretaceous
Found: Canada (Alberta)

Struthiomimus
(strooth-ee-uh-MY-mus)

Because scientists thought this dinosaur looked like an ostrich, they called it Struthiomimus, which means "ostrich mimic." It had a short body, a long tail, and a curving neck. Its head was small, it had no teeth, and its eyes were quite large. Scientists think that it may have been fairly intelligent, compared to most other dinosaurs. Struthiomimus probably lived on open river banks, pacing around for a juicy morsel. It might have caught some of the many kinds of water life that lived in the late Cretaceous. Perhaps instead it used its strong, curved claws to tear open insect nests or eggs.

This dinosaur was a member of the family of *Ornithomimus*, which belonged to the broad group of "hollow-tail lizards," or coelurosaurs. Other members of the family included *Dromiceiomimus*, *Elaphrosaurus*, and *Gallimimus*.

Length: 11 feet, 6 inches
Weight: 220 pounds
Lived: Late Cretaceous
Found: United States (New Jersey), Canada (Alberta)

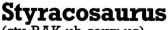

Styracosaurus
(sty-RAK-uh-sawr-us)

This is one of the most dramatic members of the short-frilled, "horned dinosaur" family. It was related to *Brachyceratops*, *Centrosaurus*, *Ceratops*, *Eoceratops*, *Monoclonius*, *Pachyrhinosaurus*, and *Triceratops*. Each of these animals had a different arrangement of horns and frills made of bone. Seen from head on, Styracosaurus was a fearsome beast. It had a long head with six large spikes that were attached to the back of its neck frill. There was a long horn on its nose and a curved beak for tearing stubborn roots or tree trunks.

Styracosaurus was probably about 6 feet tall and would have weighed around 3 tons. Scientists have calculated that it could have reached a speed of more than 20 MPH in full charge. In some ways it was the equivalent of today's rhinoceros, but much stronger and more dangerous. For all its frightening appearance, however, it was little more than half the size of *Triceratops*.

Length: 18 feet
Weight: 3 tons
Lived: Late Cretaceous
Found: United States (Montana), Canada (Alberta)

Syntarsus
(sin-TAR-sus)

This strange dinosaur was found in southern Africa. It dates back to the earliest period of the dinosaur age. Most pieces of the skeleton were found, and experts have put together a good picture of how it must have looked. The bones in its hands look similar to those from *Coelophysis*, and the two lived at about the same time. Syntarsus's foot bones, however, look more like those from a member of the *Heterodontosaurus* family. Its ankle bones look very primitive. They are fused together and not well developed. Scientists wanted to show dinosaurs with feathers and plumes on their heads, so they drew pictures of Syntarsus this way. Today, very few scientists think it had those features. It would have been surprising to have found feathers on a member of the Coelophysis family. Syntarsus had sharp teeth in its pointed mouth. It was probably quite fast and could run after small mammals and large insects.

Length: 10 feet
Weight: 65 pounds
Lived: Late Triassic
Found: Zimbabwe

Tarbosaurus
(TAR-bo-sawr-us)

One of the great flesh-eating dinosaurs of the late Cretaceous, Tarbosaurus is almost identical to *Tyrannosaurus*. Unlike its close relative, however, Tarbosaurus comes from the Nemegt Desert in Mongolia. Fossil remains from seven animals were dug up in the 1950s by a team of scientists from Russia. Later, six more skeletons were found by a Polish team. If remains had been found near *Tyrannosaurus* bones in North America, it would have been included with that family. Instead, with remains found halfway around the world, scientists have put it in a family of its own. Tarbosaurus had very short arms with two fingers and two-inch claws. Each foot had three large toes, each with a claw 4 inches long. On its back legs, Tarbosaurus would have stood more than 14 feet tall. Its powerful skull was joined together in segments. When it rammed an object to stun or kill it, the bones in its head would not crack under the shock.

Length: 33 feet
Weight: 4 tons
Lived: Late Cretaceous
Found: Mongolia

Tarchia
(TAR-kee-a)

This heavily armored dinosaur belonged to the group known as ankylosaurids, named after the giant *Ankylosaurus*. Of all the different dinosaur families in this group, Tarchia was second in size only to *Ankylosaurus*. Its name is taken from the Mongolian word for "brain." When it was found in Mongolia, the first part discovered was its brain. The very thick bone covering its head would have stood up well to charging meat eaters. Predators would have just as hard a time getting through Tarchia's thick armored body.

These were grazing animals. They were built to move around slowly without having to run away to escape attack. In that way, they were designed like giant, armored eating machines. Tarchia had a very broad snout with a wide mouth. It had a beak-like upper jaw and very small, weak teeth. With two bony horns jutting out from its skull, its head must have resembled a cow's.

Length: 28 feet
Weight: 3 tons
Lived: Late Cretaceous
Found: Mongolia (Gobi Desert)

Tenontosaurus
(ten-ON-tuh-sawr-us)

Scientists are not sure which group this dinosaur belongs in. Some classify it as a member of the *Iguanodon* family, but other scientists think it should be linked with *Hypsilophodon*. Like *Iguanodon* it was large, with a thick tail held rigid when running. Its tail was much longer than its body, and it had long front legs. This would have made it fast when moving on all fours. Unlike *Iguanodon*, it had no spikes on its thumbs. Also, it had teeth similar to *Hypsilophodon*.

Remains of Tenontosaurus have been found in Montana, Oklahoma, Texas, and Arizona. Its name means "tendon lizard" and was so given because of strong tendons, or cords, connecting bones in its backbone and tail. Tenontosaurus may have been prey to hunting packs of *Deinonychus*. Its bones have been found with these small, flesh-eating predators.

Tenontosaurus was without any real protection from bony plates or armor. It may have had little means of fighting back, and could have done nothing but run away if challenged by a predator. It is difficult to explain why some heavily protected dinosaurs lived only a short time while others without protection lived for long periods. One factor may have been the places where each lived. Members of the Iguanodon and Hypsilophodon families have been found all over the world and would have lived among some of history's most vicious predators. Both families were strong and very successful. They survived throughout the Cretaceous period. Whichever family Tenontosaurus belonged to, it was a survivor!

Length: 21 feet, 3 inches
Weight: 1 ton
Lived: Early Cretaceous
Found: United States (Montana, Oklahoma, Texas, Arizona)

Teratosaurus
(teh-RAT-uh-sawr-us)

Members of this family were the first of the big meat-eating carnosaurs, or "flesh lizards." They emerged around 200 million years ago, at the dawn of the dinosaur age. About 100 million years later, the big carnosaurs like *Tenontosaurus* and *Tyrannosaurus* would appear to scavenge the earth. Dinosaurs like Teratosaurus, however, were much faster and more agile than their giant, lumbering descendents. Teratosaurus was found in West Germany. Others from the same family have been found in England and Africa.

Teratosaurus had a large head, a strong neck, and a short body. It had fangs in its mouth and claws on its fingers and toes. Each arm had three fingers and each foot had four toes. Compare this arrangement with dinosaurs like *Tyrannosaurus* and *Tenontosaurus*, which had almost lost the use of their arms.

Length: 20 feet
Weight: 1,500 pounds
Lived: Late Triassic
Found: West Germany, England, Africa

Thecodontosaurus
(thee-kuh-DON-tuh-sawr-us)

This dinosaur was named in 1843 from a piece of jaw found in Bristol, England. Its name means "socket toothed lizard," and it had teeth set in sockets like thecodonts. Thecodonts were a group of reptiles that appeared in the Triassic period about 220 million years ago. They are believed by many scientists to have been the ancestors of all the dinosaurs, the crocodiles, the alligators, and the birds. Thecodontosaurus was a very early dinosaur of the prosauropod group. As such, it was an ancestor of the big, four-footed plant eaters.

With longer back legs than front legs, and narrow feet and hands, Thecondontosaurus would have been relatively swift on all fours. It had short neck bones and a longer hand than another relative, *Anchisaurus*. Dinosaurs of this group probably hunted in upland areas and may have stood up on their back legs to run away from danger or sprint after their prey. *Plateosaurus* was a slightly earlier member of the same group.

Length: 7 feet
Weight: ?
Lived: Late Triassic/Early Jurassic
Found: West-central England, South Africa, northeast Australia

Thescelosaurus
(THESS-uh-ol-sawr-us)

These could have been the very last dinosaurs to appear on earth before all dinosaurs disappeared permanently, around 65 million years ago. When Thescelosaurus appeared, the group to which it belonged had already existed for 80 million years or more. Thescelosaurus was related to the family of *Hypsilophodon*. Its name means "marvelous lizard" and refers to the fine condition of the fossil. Some scientists think this dinosaur bridges a gap between two large family groups. Bigger and more robust than *Hypsilophodon*, it is also built a lot like the *Iguanodon* family.

Thescelosaurus lived in North America. It had strong legs and relatively long arms. There were five toes on each foot and five fingers on each hand. These toes and fingers would have helped it run fast on two legs and claw at the ground for food. Along its back for protection were several rows of bony studs. Its pointed face had teeth in the top jaw like *Hypsilophodon*. Unlike its relative's teeth however, both sides of Thescelosaurus's teeth were coated with enamel.

Length: 11 feet
Weight: ?
Lived: Late Cretaceous
Found: United States (Montana, Wyoming), Canada (Alberta, Saskatchewan)

Torosaurus
(TOR-o-sawr-us)

A member of the family of long-frilled horned dinosaurs, Torosaurus was the largest in the group. Relatives like *Anchiceratops*, *Chasmosaurus*, and *Pentaceratops* were older and smaller. Torosaurus means "piercing lizard." The name is appropriate for Torosaurus because of its three horns. Two large horns grew from the top of its head; a third, smaller horn was on top of its nose. Torosaurus has been discovered in Wyoming, Texas, and Alberta. In all these places, only the upper jaw and the huge bone frill have been discovered. Scientists estimate that the skull and frill were almost 8 feet long.

The Torosaurus fossils tell scientists that the animal suffered from bone cancer. Although tens of millions of years separate them, this cancer is similar to that found among the bones of prehistoric Indians. Unlike *Triceratops*, the big, short-frilled dinosaur that existed on earth at the same time, Torosaurus had a smooth frill without bony studs or rough edges. This was one of the last members of the horned family and also one of the last dinosaurs to appear.

Length: 25 feet
Weight: 8 tons
Lived: Late Cretaceous
Found: United States (Texas, Wyoming, Montana), Canada (Alberta)

Triceratops
(try-SAIR-uh-tops)

Along with giant meat eaters like *Tyrannosaurus*, Triceratops is probably one of the most famous dinosaurs ever found. It has been fully examined by scientists, thanks to the discovery of a large bed of skeletons in western Wyoming. Along with *Torosaurus*, Triceratops is one of the last of the large group of horned dinosaurs called ceratopsians. Its name comes from the Greek name for three large horns.

Triceratops had a relatively short frill, especially when compared with that of *Torosaurus*. The frill had no holes to make the bone lighter, as some others did. It did have small bumpy pieces of bone on the back edge of the frill. The skull and frill together span a length of more than 6 feet. The two main horns are each more than 3 feet long.

Animals of this family would have been well-protected by their thick, leathery skin and their bony head decoration. They were probably quite slow-moving and would have used their horns more for wrestling than for charging their enemy.

Length: 30 feet
Weight: 6 tons
Lived: Late Cretaceous
Found: United States (Montana, Wyoming, South Dakota), Canada (Alberta)

Tsintaosaurus
(chin-TAY-o-sawr-us)

This was one of the last of the crested duckbills to appear on earth before all dinosaurs became extinct. Very unusual, it is of particular interest to scientists. It was found in China, and its name means "Chinese lizard." Some people think Tsintaosaurus was a descendent of *Sauroplophus*. The bony knob on the top of a *Sauroplophus* skull looks like a primitive form of the main crest on Tsintaosaurus.

Because its crest is so unusual, scientists want to know if it was used for show or developed by nature for fighting. The crest is known to have been a hollow tube. Many crested dinosaurs had hollow tubes that were probably used for making loud, booming sounds. Tsintaosaurus may have had a flap of skin stretching from its beak to the top of the crest. This would have been for show. Many animals develop parts of their body for frightening away enemies or attracting other members of their kind.

Length: 33 feet
Weight: 4 tons
Lived: Late Cretaceous
Found: China

Tuojiangosaurus
(too-HWANG-o-sawr-us)

Because it was found in the Tuojing area of China, this dinosaur is named Tuojiangosaurus, or "Tuojing lizard." Scientists only described it fully for the first time in 1977. It has been firmly placed with the family group headed by *Stegosaurus*. It is not as big, however. With a short neck and a low head, dinosaurs like these were slow-moving browsers. They had reasonably long legs and a stiffened tail.

Tuojiangosaurus had two rows of bony plates set on either side of its backbone. Altogether, 15 pairs of plates were set side by side. This arrangement was well developed and is more advanced than the arrangement seen on *Stegosaurus*. The plates protected Tuojiangosaurus from tall flesh eaters. On its tail it had a set of four bony spikes in two rows. Scientists once thought these animals were limited to the Jurassic period. Recently, though, fossils have also been found from the Cretaceous period.

Length: 23 feet
Weight: 2 tons
Lived: Early Cretaceous
Found: China (Sinkiang Province)

Tyrannosaurus
(tye-RAN-uh-sawr-us)

This is certainly the biggest meat eater and may have been the most frightening dinosaur. It was more than 40 feet long and would have stood more than 18 feet tall on its huge back legs. Its strong tail probably helped balance the animal as it lunged forward and crashed into its prey. Its head was massive and very strong. In the specimens available, some back bones were welded together. This would have resulted from collisions to the head, which then sent enormous shocks down its back. Before the bones welded, the dinosaur would have suffered terrible pain from arthritis.

With legs like giant pillars, Tyrannosaurus would have had a top speed of nearly 20 MPH. It could have kept up this pace for only short distances, though. Probably, it lay in wait for easy prey and gave a short chase. After finally crashing into its next meal, it stunned it with a massive blow from its head. Then Tyrannosaurus would kill its prey with a bone-crushing bite from its huge jaws. Its 3-foot jaws held 60 teeth, each shaped like a dagger and up to 6 inches in length.

Length: 39 feet
Weight: 7 tons
Lived: Late Cretaceous
Found: Western North America

Velociraptor
(veh-loss-ih-RAP-tor)

Velociraptor means "swift plunderer," and this dinosaur was very likely just that. Lightly built for speed and agility, it had a long, low head and a flat skull. Although some of its relatives, including *Dromaeosaurus* and *Deinonychus*, have been found in North America, Velociraptor comes from Mongolia. The shape of its head and mouth suggests that it was a variety of coelurosaur ("hollow-tailed lizard") that developed around the diet it got. One skeleton has been found with its hands clutching the head of a *Protoceratops*. Both dinosaurs seemed to have died in this final fight to the end.

Velociraptor had long fingers, each with a large claw. This would have made it efficient at killing its prey before eating it. Each foot had four toes. The "big" toe was turned in, the first toe had a large claw and the other two were used for standing on. It could run quite fast and probably lived and hunted alone.

Length: 6 feet
Weight: ?
Lived: Late Cretaceous
Found: Mongolia, China

Vulcanodon
(vul-CAN-o-don)

Called "volcano tooth" after the rock from which it was dug in Zimbabwe, Africa, this dinosaur was a large plant eater. It lived during the early Jurassic at about the same time as *Barapasaurus*. In fact, it is a member of the family group to which *Barapasaurus* belongs. Some scientists think it is a member of the prosauropod group because it has similar hips. Prosauropods developed from the ancestors of dinosaurs and lived before the really big plant eaters, called sauropods.

Vulcanodon had thick legs and a long neck and tail. No skull has ever been found, so that part of its body must be guessed at. Scientists compare Vulcanodon's bones with those of similar dinosaurs and assume that its head also resembled their heads. Most people agree that Vulcanodon is one of the very first sauropod dinosaurs. It is an ancestor of a very long line of prehistoric animals that survived until all dinosaurs, all over the world, finally became extinct.

Length: 20 feet
Weight: ?
Lived: Early Jurassic
Found: Zimbabwe

DINOSAUR SIZES

PLATEOSAURUS

DASPLETOSAURUS

COELURUS

STEGOSAURUS

TRICERATOPS

COMPSOGNATHUS

From the giant Diplodocus to the tiny Compsognathus, dinosaurs came in all shapes and sizes. Here dinosaurs are compared with modern animals like the elephant, the hippopotamus, the rhinoceros, the giraffe, the dog and man. Compare the size of Tyrannosaurus with a rhinoceros and see how Triceratops would have looked to a man!

Many dinosaurs, like Coelurus were fast, nimble and hard to catch. Others, like Diplodocus were slow, lumbering animals rather like the modern elephant. Stegosaurus, like the rhinoceros, was well protected and could probably run quite fast too. What a strange sight it would be if all these animals could really be seen around today!

HIPPOPOTAMUS

ELEPHANT

TYRANNOSAURUS

RHINOCEROS

DIPLODOCUS

GIRAFFE

MAN

DOG

TERMS TO REMEMBER

Ankylosaurs — "Fused lizard" dinosaurs with heavy bodies, short limbs and protective armor.

Carnosaurs — Means "flesh lizard"; the large and powerful flesh-eating dinosaurs.

Ceratopsian — "Horned dinosaurs," which were among the last to appear and among the most abundant of all dinosaur groups. A type with large beaks and neck frills.

Coelurosaurs — Means "hollow-tailed lizard"; a group of 16 separate dinosaur families, all of which were small and lightly built.

Cretaceous — The most recent period of the Mesozoic, generally considered to have begun 135 million years ago and to have ended 65 million years ago.

Jurassic — The middle period of the Mesozoic, generally considered to have begun 190 million years ago and to have ended 135 million years ago.

Mammals — A class of higher vertebrates including man and other animals that nourish their young with milk secreted by mammary glands and are usually more or less covered with hair.

Mesozoic — Comes from the Greek meaning "middle life" and refers to the geologic period between the Paleozoic and the Cenozoic. The Mesozoic is divided into three periods: the Triassic, the Jurassic and the Cretaceous.

Ornithopods — "Bird feet" dinosaurs capable of walking on their back legs.

Ornithischian — A member of the bird-hipped group of dinosaurs.

Paleontology — The science of dealing with past life from early geologic records and fossil remains.

Prosauropods — Means literally "before the lizard feet" dinosaurs, or Sauropods.

Pterosaurs — Bird-like "winged lizards" which were not dinosaurs at all but a group of animals capable of gliding long distances.

Reptiles — Animals that crawl or move on their belly or on short legs. The body is usually covered with scales or bony plates.

Sauropods — The family of "lizard feet" dinosaurs which included some of the largest animals known to have lived.

Saurischian — A member of the lizard-hipped group of dinosaurs.

Stegosaurs — "Roof lizard," or plated, dinosaurs with bones or spikes protruding through thick skin.

Thecodontians — Socket-toothed reptiles that first appeared about 230 million years ago are thought to have given way to the dinosaurs.

Triassic — The earliest period of the Mesozoic, generally considered to have b[...] million years ago and ended 190 million years ago.